Key Concepts in Adult Education and Training
2nd Edition

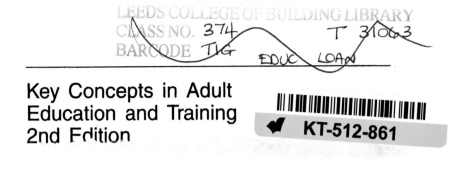

This book is an accessible and jargon-free guide to the key concepts used in adult education and training. The author examines in detail forty-five of these concepts, ranging from core concepts such as education and development to more specialist concepts like social capital and social inclusion. This new edition has been fully revised and updated in view of the recent surge of interest in concepts such as lifelong education and the learning society.

All those involved in the field of adult education and training come into contact with specialist ideas or concepts on a daily basis. This book is designed for students and practitioners of adult education and training who wish to develop their understanding of these many associated concepts. At the end of each chapter there is also an annotated list of useful books or articles for those who would like to investigate particular concepts in more detail.

Malcolm Tight is Professor of Education at the University of Warwick. He has published widely in the field of post-compulsory education and is the Editor of the journal *Studies in Higher Education*.

Key Concepts in Adult Education and Training
2nd Edition

Malcolm Tight

RoutledgeFalmer
Taylor & Francis Group

LONDON AND NEW YORK

First published 1996 by Routledge

Reprinted 1998, 2000

Second edition first published 2002
by RoutledgeFalmer
2 Park Square, Milton Park, Abingdon, Oxon, OX14 4RN

Simultaneously published in the USA and Canada
by RoutledgeFalmer
270 Madison Ave, New York NY 10016

RoutledgeFalmer is an imprint of the Taylor & Francis Group

Transferred to Digital Printing 2005

© 1996, 2002 Malcolm Tight

Typeset in Palatino by
Florence Production Ltd, Stoodleigh, Devon

British Library Cataloguing in Publication Data
A catalogue record for this book is available from the
British Library

Library of Congress Cataloging in Publication Data
A catalog record for this book has been requested

ISBN 0–415–27579–2

*For Christina
with all my love*

Contents

Figures

Introduction

CONCEPTS IN ADULT EDUCATION AND TRAINING

Adult education and training – now widely re-labelled and re-energized under the banner of lifelong learning (see Chapter 2) – is an important and developing field of activity and study. We are all, as children and as adults, engaged in learning every day of our lives, whether we realize it or not. We are also increasingly likely to be involved in more formalized forms of learning – that is, in education or training – both immediately after we have completed the compulsory education period and throughout the rest of our lives.

Many thousands of us are currently employed to assist and guide the learning of other adults: as teachers or trainers, as lecturers or facilitators, as advisors or managers. We may be employed as such full-time or part-time, or this role may form only one part of a more general portfolio of supervisory responsibilities. We may work in a designated institution of education or training. We may work for other public, private or voluntary sector organizations, which have a concern for the development of their employees or members. Or we may work on our own account and need to update our skills and knowledge.

Every year, large numbers of those involved in the education and training of adults themselves undertake some form of education or training to support or prepare them for these roles. This professional development may take place at a variety of levels, leading to, for example, a teaching certificate, a first degree, a professional qualification or a research degree. Or it may not involve any qualification at all, and may indeed be entirely self-directed.

All who study or research adult education and training, or are involved in its delivery, will come into contact with many ideas or concepts that are of importance to the field. If they are studying for a relevant qualification, they will probably have to write essays or assignments about these concepts. More commonly, they will be expected to have a general under-standing of their meaning, applicability and inter-relationships.

This book is designed for people in these positions, who have some responsibility for, and/or interest in, adult education and training, and who wish to develop their understanding of the many associated concepts. Written in an accessible and relatively jargon-free style, it contains plentiful references for those who would like to investigate particular concepts in more detail.

The book aims to offer a map of the field and a framework for further study. It certainly does not seek to provide the last word: whole books could be written about any of the concepts discussed here, and, as the references indicate, they have been! Neither does it offer the kind of conceptual analysis practised by philosophers or linguists for other philosophers or linguists. The style of writing, while critical and demanding, is intended to both demystify and encourage interest on a broader front.

A CONTESTED TERRAIN

What, then, are concepts? In essence, they are labels for ideas that are of key importance to us. Examples from general conver-sation would include truth and beauty, good and evil, happiness and hunger, love and destiny. Concepts have, therefore, a reso-nance that can go beyond that of more ordinary words. This resonance depends crucially, of course, upon their context. Thus, words that are key concepts for adult educators and trainers may just be ordinary words for others, and vice-versa. The same is true within the field of adult education and training, so that different practitioners or participants will emphasize different concepts and apply them in different ways.

From this brief account, it will be apparent that particular concepts may not have the same meaning or meanings for all. Indeed, it is a characteristic of concepts that their interpretation and usage varies: in other words, they are contested. They may be accorded varied meanings by different interest groups, includ-ing individual educators or trainers, professional organizations, employers and trades unions, central and local government, and international agencies. They will be employed in these ways in what academics term 'discourses', in which '[k]nowledge is held to be partial and contingent upon the specific factors and contexts within which it is constructed and presented' (Edwards 1997, p. 5).

Thus, understandings of concepts will vary across time and space. Historically, concepts may come and go as policy imperatives and fashions change. Some will retain their underlying importance, though their interpretation and coverage may change. Some may be reinvented from time to time, but given new labels. In spatial terms, the meaning and significance of concepts may vary from country to country, and region to region, even from town to town. Thus, it is common to find different terms used – or the same terms used differently – in, for example, industrialized and developing nations, and in anglophone and francophone countries.

At this point, it has to be recognized that the terms used to label this book, 'adult', 'education' and 'training', are themselves contested concepts (and they will be considered as such in Chapter 1). The field of adult education and training remains broad, fractured and amorphous, differently understood, labelled and defined in different countries and by different interests. This variation and contestation is apparent from the scope, and also constitutes one of the main themes, of this book. We work in a contested terrain.

QUESTIONS OF VALUES

There is also, of course, a personal dimension. This book has no pretensions to objectivity, neutrality or balance. It offers the interpretation of one middle-aged, middle-class, able-bodied, white English man, who has been working in various capacities in the field of adult education and training for more than twenty years. The organization of the book, the selection of the concepts for discussion and the views expressed are all in essence my own. Many other authors are, of course, referred to, but their ideas are mediated through my presentation and critique.

Other writers would undoubtedly have chosen a different selection of concepts and authors and would have stressed a different collection of points. Indeed, I would have produced a different book if I had written it at a different time, as anyone can see if they care to compare the first and second editions. The motivation for writing the book came largely from the perceived lack of a book of this nature, which I would have found a useful resource. Its writing has been a learning journey for me, as I hope it will be for many readers in their turn.

So it may be useful to say something here relating to my own preferences, biases and values, at least in-so-far as I am aware of them, which the reader will then find reflected throughout the book. I would identify the following as most relevant to the present context:

- I try to take a broad view of what constitutes adult education and training, and would rather go beyond borders than confine myself within them.
- I regard adult education and training essentially as a field of practice, not as a discipline. As such, I see the work of many disciplines as being relevant to it.
- I consider myself a generalist rather than a specialist or an expert.
- I am at least as much interested in the relations between concepts as in their distinctive characteristics.
- I like to avoid jargon wherever possible (though concepts are, of course, at one level, jargon) and present the discussion in ways that should be widely intelligible.
- As already stated, I am a middle-aged, middle-class, able-bodied, white English man. As such, while I may try to take account of the perspectives of others of different age, class, ability, ethnicity, nationality and gender, I have not experienced these perspectives.
- All of the books and articles referred to in this book are written in the English language, or have been translated into English.
- The majority of the material discussed originates, therefore, from the United Kingdom, North America and Australasia.
- Finally, recognizing these preferences, limitations and reservations, I have, nevertheless, endeavoured to produce a book which is as generally useful as possible.

With this brief venture into the first person completed, I will now slip back into the third person, with which, as an academic, I am naturally rather happier.

ORGANIZATION OF THE BOOK

The first edition of this book (Tight 1996) came together through a combination of top–down and bottom–up strategies. In other words, while there was a clear plan at the beginning, there were significant changes made during its production, in terms of both overall structure and of what was, and was not, included. This occurred despite the fact that the book was essentially written in a relatively short, three-month, period. Indeed, as already suggested, writing the book was an illuminating and fruitful learning experience for the author.

Core Concepts	adult, education, training, learning, teaching, development
International Concepts	lifelong, learning organization, the learning society
Institutional Concepts	further and higher, adult and continuing, community, formal, non-formal, informal
Work-related Concepts	human capital, human resource development, career, professional, social capital
Learning Concepts	distance, open, flexible, experiential, problem-based, independent, self-directed, andragogy, conscientization, communities of practice
Curricular Concepts	knowledge and skill, capability and enterprise, competence, quality
Structural Concepts	access and participation, accreditation and modularization, success and dropout, social inclusion

Figure I.1 The organization of the book

The organization of the book is summarized in Figure I.1. From this, as from the Contents, it can be seen that the 45 concepts discussed have been grouped into seven chapters. While this organization was both carefully considered and, to some extent, original, the concepts might well have been grouped and labelled differently. Similarly, other concepts could have been discussed – indeed, many are referred to in passing in the body of the text – and some of those that are discussed could have been left out.

With one exception, there is no particular significance to the ordering of the chapters. What have been referred to as the core concepts (see the next section) are discussed first; the remaining chapters could have been placed in almost any order. As the reader will note, many cross-references have been made between the chapters in an attempt to illuminate the relationships between the concepts discussed.

It would, of course, have been possible to organize the book in a dictionary or encyclopedia format, with the concepts discussed in alphabetical order. They have, however, been linked together in groups of some coherence, so as to allow a more comparative, linked and flowing discussion. The labels used to identify the groups and chapters – core, international, institutional, work-related, learning, curricular, structural – are not, however, put forward as in any way definitive. They are my own conceptualization and basically a suggestive convenience.

WHAT'S NEW ABOUT THE SECOND EDITION?

This second edition of the book is a fairly straightforward revision of the first edition. In undertaking the revision, two main kinds of change have been made. First, new references, quotations and examples have been included to update the text, with some of the older ones from the first edition replaced or removed. Indeed, of the 450 or so references in this edition, some 30 per cent date from after the first edition was written. Second, some new concepts, or concepts that have come to assume greater importance to the field, have been added. These include social capital (Chapter 4), problem-based learning and communities of practice (Chapter 5), and social inclusion (Chapter 7). So the new edition is a bit longer than the original.

In preparing the second edition, I have been particularly struck by two things. One is the great ferment of interest in a number of concepts generated since the first edition was published. I am thinking here particularly of the linked concepts of lifelong education, the learning society and two newcomers, social capital and social inclusion (discussed further in the section on conceptual pasts and futures in Chapter 8). The other is the increased extent to which concepts discussed in different chapters appear to be interrelated. This tendency seemed so strong that I was tempted to substantially revise the organization of the book. In the end, though, I resisted this temptation and opted instead to increase the number of cross-references.

Only one concept has been deleted for this edition, though I was tempted in a number of other cases that now seem somewhat historical (and will probably delete them if there is a third edition of this book). The deleted concept was recurrent education, once a rival to lifelong learning/education, but now absorbed by it and rarely referred to.

CORE AND QUALIFYING CONCEPTS

Chapter 1 focuses on what I have termed the *core* concepts. In other words, these are the concepts that are the most common and central, and therefore, the most essential to an understanding of the field. They include the three concepts included in the title of the book – adult, education and training – plus the related ideas of learning, teaching and development.

Chapters 2 to 7 then examine what, by contrast, may be termed *qualifying* concepts. These concepts refer to approaches to, or details of, the field as defined by the core concepts. Indeed, it is commonly the case in practice that concepts are presented as two words – one qualifying, one core – as in the cases of, for example, lifelong learning, higher education, skill development, distance teaching or professional training. This relationship is illustrated in Figure I.2.

In Figure I.2, the words to the right of the vertical line are the core concepts, while those to the left are the qualifying concepts. The bulk of the concepts discussed in detail in Chapters 2 to 7 have been listed on the left-hand side. In the great majority of cases, further concepts can be created by combining any of the words on the left with any of those on the right. Most of these combinations have an existing usage; even where they do not, they usually still make sense.

Lifelong	
Further	
Higher	
Adult	
Continuing	
Community	
Formal	
Informal	
Non-formal	
Human resource	**Education**
Career	**Training**
Professional	**Learning**
Distance	**Teaching**
Open	
Flexible	**Development**
Experiential	
Problem-based	
Independent	
Self-directed	
Knowledge	
Skill	
Capability	
Enterprise	
Competence	
Quality	

Figure 1.2 Core and qualifying concepts

The major exception to this relationship appears to be the group of terms discussed in Chapter 7 under the label of 'structural concepts': access and participation, accreditation and modularization, success and dropout, and social inclusion. The reason for this difference seems clear. The other chapters are largely concerned with examining what are, at least in part, approaches to adult education and training: e.g. community, competence, flexible or career education, training, learning, teaching or development. In Chapter 7, however, the focus is more on the internal organization of such approaches.

FRAMEWORKS FOR ANALYSIS

How do we, or should we, go about the analysis of concepts? Philosophers and linguists, as already mentioned, have long had their own techniques of conceptual analysis (see, for example, Flew 1956). While what is presented in this book could legitimately also be termed conceptual analysis, it is not approached from an overly philosophical point of view. Rather, the aim has been to make use of a number of alternative frameworks for analysis, drawing on a variety of disciplinary traditions.

The analytical frameworks that suggest themselves for these purposes include, where relevant:

- the history and development of the concepts discussed;
- their disciplinary origins and location (e.g. biology, economics, history, management, philosophy, politics, psychology, sociology);
- their national and international policy context, and their usage in different countries;
- their treatment of underlying social variables (e.g. gender, class, race, age);
- their relevance to different levels of activity (e.g. individual, organization, society);
- their linkages with, and relations to, each other.

These frameworks will be utilized in each of the chapters that follow to illustrate the background, application and wider context of the concepts discussed. The final chapter, Chapter 8, will then attempt an overall evaluation of the concepts examined, of the frameworks used to analyse them, and of what this tells us about the field of study.

HOW TO USE THIS BOOK

A little guidance on how to use this book may be of assistance to some readers. It is not envisaged that many readers will wish, or feel the need, to read all of the way through the book, certainly not at one sitting. The most probable and useful strategy for most will be to focus on those chapters that cover areas or concepts of particular interest. These can be identified through the Contents or the index, or just by browsing through the text.

In most cases, however, readers will likely have something to gain from a study of the Introduction and the concluding chapter. These provide a general framework for considering, and some conclusions on, the use of concepts in adult education and training.

A FEW FINAL POINTS

Three points remain to be made before this introductory chapter is concluded. First, it is common practice in some circles to place concepts under discussion in quotation marks: thus, 'education', 'self-directed' and so forth. This has not been adopted as standard practice in this book, but has only been used where it seemed necessary to help intelligibility. To do otherwise would have been to clutter the book with quotation marks, and possibly both confuse and irritate the reader.

Second, as the earlier discussion of core and qualifying concepts will have made apparent, this book is not simply an examination of 45 free-standing concepts. It is also, at least implicitly, an analysis of the more than 150 concepts that can be made by combining the different core and qualifying concepts. It would have been wasteful and tedious, however, to keep referring to all of these possible permutations in the text. Instead, the core concepts have been used in Chapters 2 to 7 in an almost interchangeable fashion. Thus, where, for example, non-formal education is being examined, the discussion is also meant to encompass non-formal learning, non-formal training, non-formal development and non-formal teaching, unless explicitly stated to the contrary.

Third, and finally, as the reader who has already browsed through the book will have noted, the discussion is extensively referenced. This has been done in two ways, with the aim of making the book as useful to the reader as possible. At the end of each chapter, except this one and Chapter 8, you will find a selected and annotated list of some of the most useful and accessible books or articles which cover the concepts discussed there. A much more comprehensive set of references is given at the end of the book for those who wish to explore particular discussions somewhat further.

Chapter 1

The Core Concepts

OPPOSITIONAL OR RELATED TERMS?

This chapter examines six basic terms. Three of them – adult, education and training – form the title of this book. The other three – learning, teaching and development – are closely related. Together, these six terms can be seen as providing the baseline of core concepts that define, in complementary and competing ways, the breadth and nature of the field of study. The final section of the chapter looks at what has been one of the key debates in this field over many years, that between liberal and vocational emphases on education and training. Chapters 2 to 7 then analyse an extensive range of qualifying concepts (for an explanation of the distinction between 'core' and 'qualifying' concepts, see the Introduction), which are widely used in association with the core concepts to signify narrower areas of interest.

As core concepts, the six terms examined in this chapter have naturally been widely discussed. Such discussion is commonly organized in terms of oppositions or dichotomies, or of inclusion and exclusion. Thus, education and training may be seen as opposing terms, the former broad, knowledge-based and general, the latter narrow, skill-based and specific (see also the discussion of knowledge and skill in Chapter 6). Indeed, this kind of approach is another representation of the liberal versus vocational debate reviewed in the final section of this chapter. Similarly, learning may be seen in opposition to teaching, the one receptive and perhaps passive (but see the examination of self-directed learning in Chapter 5), the other directive and organizational.

Analyses based on the idea of inclusion or exclusion quite often make use of diagrams, with the concepts discussed portrayed as circles or ovals. In such cases, training may be represented as a small oval wholly contained within a larger oval labelled education, which itself is completely enclosed within an even larger oval circle learning. Or, combining the idea of opposition with that of inclusion/exclusion, education and training may be shown as overlapping ovals (see Figure 1.1). This presentation illustrates the idea that, while some learning activities may definitively be termed either education or training, in between there is a larger or smaller group of activities which might legitimately be called either or both.

While such presentations may be criticized as inevitably rather simplistic, they do, nevertheless, demonstrate differing but widely held views or perceptions. This chapter aims to go a little deeper.

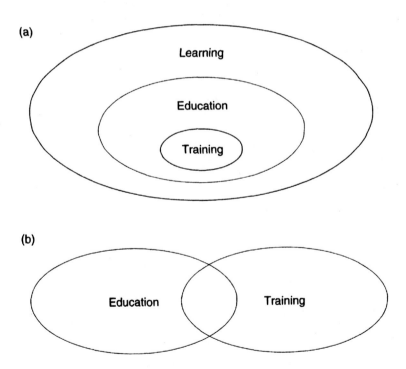

(a)

Learning

Education

Training

(b)

Education　　　Training

Figure 1.1 Alternative diagrammatic representations of core conceptual relations

ADULT

What do we mean when we call someone an adult? What distinguishes adult education, adult training and adult learning from education, training and learning in a more general sense? The second of these questions has an institutional or organizational context, and is discussed further in Chapter 3 (see the section on adult and continuing, p. 62). The former question will be addressed in this section.

> A wide range of concepts is involved when we use the term 'adult'. The word can refer to a *stage* in the life cycle of the individual; he or she is first a child, then a youth, then an adult. It can refer to *status*, an acceptance by society that the person concerned has completed his or her novitiate and is now incorporated fully into the community. It can refer to a social *sub-set*: adults as distinct from children. Or it can include a set of *ideals and values*: adulthood.
>
> (Rogers 1996, p. 34, original emphasis)

At its simplest, adulthood may be defined purely in terms of age. Thus, in England, people may be assumed to become adult at 18 years old, when they get the right to vote. Until relatively recently, however, the voting age was 21 years, and there are many adult roles – for example, those requiring a specialist education or training – which cannot be entered into until this age or later. Similarly, some aspects of adulthood may be exercised before reaching 18 years old, such as marriage, full-time employment (including in the armed forces) and taxation.

Yet adult status is not accorded to all at these ages. Thus, those with severe disabilities may never achieve or be allowed full adult status. The age of majority also varies somewhat from country to country, or even within countries. And, whereas in industrialized countries the age of majority is legally defined, in developing countries it may be more a case of local cultural tradition. In such cases, maturity may be recognized in an essentially physical or biological sense, related to the onset or ending of puberty, and may vary in terms of age, not just for boys and girls but for individuals as well.

It would, of course, be naïve to believe that merely surviving long enough to wake up on one's eighteenth birthday, or passing through puberty, automatically changes one from being a child to being an adult. While the effects of puberty are externally recognizable, we do not (yet) wear barcodes on our sides recording our age, and other peoples' reactions to us depend, in any case, upon many factors other than our absolute age. These include, most notably, our sex and ethnicity, and the reaction will vary with the characteristics of the perceiver as well as our own.

Within industrialized countries, as Rogers (1996) indicates, we also commonly recognize an intermediary stage between childhood and adulthood. Then we may be called variously adolescents, youths or teenagers. So the transition from child to adult is not sudden or instantaneous.

The idea of 'adult' is not, therefore, directly connected to age, but is related to what generally happens as we grow older. That is, we achieve physical maturity, become capable of providing for ourselves, move away (at least in most western societies) from our parents, have children of our own, and exercise a much greater role in the making of our own choices. This then affects not just how we see ourselves, but how others see us as well. In other words, we may see the difference between being and not being an adult as chiefly being about status and self-image.

Adulthood may thus be considered as a state of being that both accords rights to individuals and simultaneously confers duties or responsibilities upon them. We might then define adulthood as: 'an ethical status resting on the presumption of various moral and personal qualities' (Paterson 1979, p. 31). Having said that, however, we also have to recognize what a heterogeneous group of people adults are. It is this amorphous group which forms the customer base or audience for adult education and training.

EDUCATION

As adults, all of us have had a considerable experience of education, though this experience may have been largely confined to our childhood, and may not be continuing. The nature of education may, therefore, seem to be relatively clear to us, with particular associations with educational institutions such as schools, colleges and universities.

Such a conceptualization – that is, that education is what takes place in educational institutions – is, however, not satisfactory for three main reasons. First, it is circular, defining each concept ('education', 'educational institution') in terms of the other. Second, it tells us nothing about the qualities of education other than its location (e.g. we might just as well define oranges as 'things that grow on orange trees'). Third, with a little thought we would probably recognize that education takes place in other kinds of institutions as well.

This final point is at the heart of the distinction between formal and non-formal education (see Chapter 3). The former is defined as taking place in educational institutions, and the latter in other kinds of institutions, the primary function of which is not education (e.g. churches, factories, health centres, prisons, military bases). It might also be pointed out that education may take place outside institutions altogether, as in the case of distance education (see the section on distance in Chapter 5), though here the association with an institution remains important.

The nature of education has been the subject of a considerable amount of analysis by philosophers of education (e.g. Barrow and White 1993, Hirst and Peters 1970, Peters 1967). Thus, Peters, in one of his more accessible works, identified three criteria for education:

(i)   that 'education' implies the transmission of what is worthwhile to those who become committed to it;
(ii) that 'education' must involve knowledge and understanding and some kind of cognitive perspective, which are not inert;
(iii) that 'education' at least rules out some procedures of transmission, on the grounds that they lack wittingness and voluntariness on the part of the learner.

(Peters 1966, p. 45)

We can critically pick away at this quotation with relative ease. Who decides what is worthwhile, for example: the learner?, the teacher?, the institution?, employers?, the state? How much time must we allow to pass in order to detect commitment? How active (i.e. not inert) do we have to be to be judged as involved in an educational activity? In what sense can children – as distinct from adults, for whom we might at least assume some degree of voluntariness if they are participating in education – be said to be voluntarily engaged in education? Yet these points confirm how useful accounts like that of Peters can be in identifying and delimiting many of the key questions we need to address in order to satisfactorily define a concept like education.

A rather simpler definition has been given by the United Nations Educational, Scientific and Cultural Organization (UNESCO). They view education as 'organized and sustained instruction designed to communicate a combination of knowledge, skills and understanding valuable for all the activities of life' (quoted in Jarvis 1990, p. 105). The key phrase here, which is not explicit in Peters' formulation, and which may be used to distinguish education from learning, appears to be 'organized and sustained instruction'. This implies the involvement of an educator of some kind, and probably also an institution, though the education might be mediated through the printed text or computer software. It also suggests that education is not a speedy process, but takes a lengthy, though perhaps not continuous, period of time. Learning, by contrast, could be seen as not necessarily involving instruction, and as often occurring over a shorter timeframe and in smaller chunks.

Clearly, distinctions of this kind are not always cut and dried. They allow us to conceive of education and learning as ends of a spectrum, and as shading into each other (see Figure 1.2a). Consequently, there will be instances that could be described quite legitimately as either education or learning or both. To some extent, therefore, the terms may be used interchangeably.

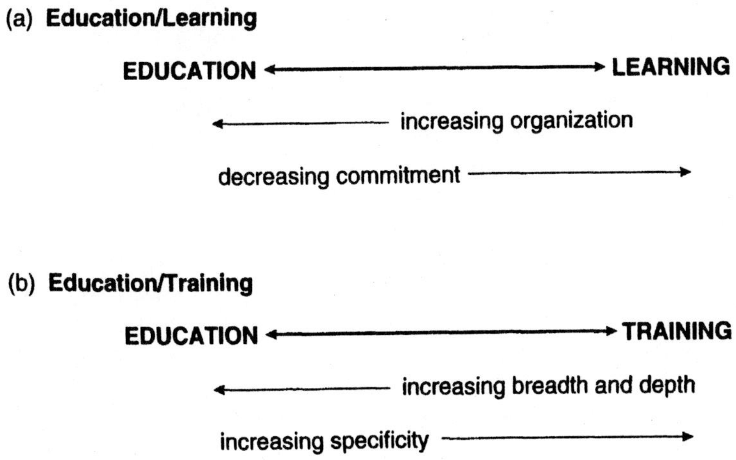

(a) **Education/Learning**

EDUCATION ←————————————————→ LEARNING

←———————— increasing organization

decreasing commitment ————————→

(b) **Education/Training**

EDUCATION ←————————————————→ TRAINING

←———————— increasing breadth and depth

increasing specificity ————————→

Figure 1.2 The education/learning and education/training spectra

How, then, to distinguish education from training? The distinction may be seen as somewhat analogous to that between education and learning, in the sense of delimiting another dimension to the area of study. The commonest approaches to making this distinction are to use the ideas of breadth and/or depth, or, conversely, to emphasize the lack of immediate application and criticality of education:

> Probably the clearest if not the only criterion of educational value . . . is that the learning in question contributes to the development of knowledge and understanding, in both breadth and depth.
>
> (Dearden 1984, p. 90)

> we need *some* conception of education as independent of immediate practical considerations – one that incorporates the ability to largely, or partly anyway, transcend the working context if necessary, and which enables people to look critically at the performance of a task or role within terms of reference not provided for them only by others, but in the light of more general and perhaps universal standards.
>
> (McKenzie 1995, p. 41)

These quotations, like the one from UNESCO, identify education as being a general rather than a specific activity. Similarly, like both the Peters and UNESCO quotations, they portray education as having to do with the development of knowledge and understanding. The latter, in particular, may be argued as being at the heart of what we mean by education:

> Use of the word 'understanding', as opposed to 'knowledge', implies that what is at issue is something more than mere information and the ability to relay or act in accordance with formulae, prescriptions and instructions (the latter is characteristic of training rather than education). An ability to recite dates, answer general knowledge quizzes, or reproduce even quite complex pieces of reasoning, is not necessary to being educated. Rather one requires of an educated person that he [sic] should have internalised information, explanation, and reasoning, and made sense of it. He should understand the principles behind the specifics that he encounters; he sets particulars in a wider frame of theoretical understanding . . . The educated person has understanding across a range of human knowledge.
>
> (Barrow and Milburn 1990, pp. 106–7)

Following these arguments, we might distinguish education from training on two grounds. First, that the former is a broader and deeper learning activity. Second, that the latter is more likely to be involved with the development of specific identified skills, while the former has to do with more general levels of understanding. Once again, though, the differences are not precise and we are left with shady areas and overlaps (see Figure 1.2b). These have become more evident in recent years with attempts to identify the transferable, core or key skills, or competencies, developed through school, further and higher educational courses (see Chapter 6).

Different approaches to understanding what is meant by education have been pursued by sociologists, focusing on its function and place within society (Blackledge and Hunt 1985). Knowledge and understanding, the avowed purposes of education, may be viewed as socially constructed rather than absolute. The educational system may be seen as an apparatus of the state, with its function being the production of people (workers) with desired skills and qualities. From this perspective, state education is, therefore, in the business of reproducing existing social and economic divisions (see, for example, Bourdieu and Passeron 1990, Bowles and Gintis 1976, Young 1998).

From such a perspective, the meaning of education cannot, of course, be properly understood in individualistic or psychological terms, but requires an appreciation of its broader social context. This context includes not just the educational and other institutions, and other settings, within which education takes place, but a consideration of their position, relationships and linkages within society. Education thus has political, economic, technological and social ramifications, and must necessarily remain a highly contested concept.

TRAINING

Training has entered the field of educational thought quite late and by the back door of professional training, as an 'inferior' form of education.

(Pineau 2000, p. 128)

The idea of training is most usually associated with preparing someone for performing a task or role, typically, but not necessarily, in a work setting (e.g. Buckley and Caple 1990, Jarvis 1990, Nadler and Nadler 1990). As such, it forms part of the broader fields of development (considered later in this chapter) and human resource development (a concept discussed in Chapter 4). It may also be seen, however, as a specific element or outcome of a more general process of education. Peters again offers a useful definition:

> The concept of 'training' has application when (i) there is some specifiable type of performance that has to be mastered, (ii) practice is required for the mastery of it, (iii) little emphasis is placed on the underlying *rationale*.
>
> (Peters 1967, p. 15, original emphasis)

This definition stresses the idea of 'mastering' the task or role, and the need for repetitive practice to enable the individual to do so, while suggesting that the actual performance might be fairly mechanical and uninformed by any underlying knowledge or understanding.

Other definitions also concern themselves with the location of the training to be undertaken:

> training is defined as the systematic acquisition of skills, rules, concepts or attitudes that result in improved performance in the work situation. In some of these instances, such as direct on-the-job training, the instructional environment is very similar if not identical to the on-the-job environment. In other instances, the training occurs in a place far removed from the actual worksite, such as a classroom.
>
> (Goldstein and Gessner 1988, p. 43)

Interestingly, this definition extends the function of training beyond the previous one, making it clear that training may be related to behaviours at least as much as to tasks. We might question here whether, if the trainer is seeking to instil concepts and attitudes, this can be effectively done without developing the trainee's underlying knowledge and understanding. While broadening its function, however, this second definition narrows the location of training, by focusing on work-related training, whether this is actually work-based or not.

A third definition makes clearer the potentially wide scope of the term:

Training typically involves instruction and practice aimed at reaching a particular level of competence or operative efficiency. As a result of training we are able to respond adequately and appropriately to some expected and typical situation. Often training addresses itself to improving performance in direct dealing with things. Thus it is necessary to train drivers and pilots, carpenters and surgeons, electricians and computer programmers. Other sorts of training are more concerned with dealing with people, as with training in sales techniques, training for supervisory positions or assertiveness training for women. Yet other kinds of training are more indirectly concerned with changing or controlling people or things, such as training to be an architect, lawyer or administrator.

(Dearden 1984, p. 59)

Dearden uses the idea of competence rather than performance (see the discussion of competence in Chapter 6). He limits the concept to preparing people to respond to common situations, while demonstrating its application to jobs of greater or lesser status. He also brings in a useful threefold typology of training to distinguish between dealing with things, with people, and with change or control. The third category includes examples that might equally be thought of as education, illustrating the potential overlap between these two key terms.

While practitioners and academics may have fairly clear, if varied, ideas about the meaning of training, these are not necessarily shared by the general public. For, though most people probably have a reasonably common understanding of the term 'education', associating it with schools, colleges, universities and other educational institutions, the same cannot be said of their views of training. A recent British study of this issue came to the following conclusions:

- that the general population uses the term training to refer to a much narrower set of activities than those understood by training professionals;
- that for most people training is that which happens in formal courses;
- that employers have a narrower definition of training than employees . . .

- that activities included in the definition of training will vary across subgroups of the population . . .
- that activities which are self-initiated and/or self-funded are less likely to be included . . .
- that for most people training is vocationally linked;
- that there is a fuzzy boundary between training and education for most people.

(Campanelli *et al.* 1994, p. 92)

The sponsors of the study in question, a government department, might well have been concerned by these findings, as it may be the case that such a lack of shared conceptual clarity is one factor limiting the development of the British vocational education and training system (see the final section of this chapter).

LEARNING

Similar issues are faced by researchers interested in the prevalence of learning amongst the general public. Thus, in 1997, two national surveys of adult learning, both sponsored by the then Department of Education and Employment, came up with very different figures for the proportion of the adult population who had been involved in some kind of learning activity during the last three years: 40 per cent (Sargant *et al.* 1997) and 75 per cent (Beinart and Smith 1997). While there were minor differences in the dates, geographical coverage and age groups targeted by the two surveys, the explanation for this difference lay:

in the differences in the definitions of learning and participation used, and in the different methods employed in administering the two surveys . . . [one] survey succeeded in being more inclusive, and in recording more information on self-directed and 'untaught' learning activities. The . . . [other] survey, by contrast, led its respondents to restrict their answers more to formal and accredited kinds of education and training.

(Tight 1998c, p. 113)

In an attempt to explore the varied understandings held by people of the terms education, learning and training, a further survey was carried out by the Campaign for Learning in 1998. This asked respondents which of a series of words and phrases they most associated with each of the three terms. It found that:

- learning was most associated with the words *discovering, finding out more, enjoyment, TV/video, exchanging ideas/information with others,* and *personal growth;*
- training was most associated with *gaining new skills, computers* and *hard work;* while
- education was most associated with *school, studying, qualifications,* and *being taught*

(Campaign for Learning 1998).

The strong apparent linkage between education and school, training and work, and learning and enjoyable discovery may seem reassuring, disconcerting or just plain predictable, depending upon your own position. Yet there was also a considerable variation and overlap in the replies, such that some respondents associated each of the words read out with learning, education and training.

A common sense view would be that learning, like breathing, is something everyone does all of the time – 'you are never too old to learn' – even if they do not realize that they are doing it. It is a fundamental human process, yet, even amongst psychologists and educators, there are many and divergent opinions about just what learning is:

The older and more traditional view of learning (the one held by Francis Bacon in 1674, for example), and the one prevalent in almost all education theory as well as in some psychological writings . . . sees learning in terms of its objectives or outcomes . . . To most classical learning theorists (for example, Pavlov, Thorndike and Skinner), however, as well as to more contemporary contributors such as Mezirow, Lovell and Schön, learning is basically a verb.

(Thomas 1991, p. 3)

There is not space, and it would not be appropriate, to review the full range of behavioural, cognitive and humanistic learning theories here (for such a review, see, for example, Cross 1981, Curzon 1997, Tennant 1997). The difference between those who regard learning as an outcome and those who see it as a process may be readily demonstrated, however, by comparing the views of two of the most prominent recent learning theorists, Gagné and Kolb.

Gagné develops a systems approach to learning and offers an information-processing model. He identifies the elements of the learning event as consisting of the learner, a stimulus situation, the learner's memory and his or her response to the stimulus. What is learned may consist of intellectual skills, verbal information, cognitive strategies, motor skills or attitudes. Different types of learning are recognized at successively higher hierarchical levels: signal learning, stimulus-response learning, motor and verbal chaining, multiple discrimination, concept learning, rule learning, problem solving. For Gagné, 'Learning is a change in human disposition or capability that persists over a period of time and is not simply ascribable to processes of growth' (1985, p. 2).

Kolb, on the other hand, builds on the work of Lewin, Dewey and Piaget. He argues that learning is best conceived as a process, not in terms of outcomes; that it is a continuous process grounded in experience; that this process requires the resolution of conflicts between different ways of looking at the world; that learning is an holistic process of adaptation to the world; that it involves transactions between the learner and the environment; and that it is the process of creating knowledge. In short, 'Learning is the process whereby knowledge is created through the transformation of experience' (Kolb 1984, p. 38).

Kolb's approach has arguably been the more influential in recent years in adult education and training, and may be seen to underlie much contemporary practice; indeed, it seems unusual these days to find a textbook or student assignment on this topic without an illustration of Kolb's (in)famous learning cycle. In this way, the emphasis in the learning process has been increasingly placed on the learners, their empowerment and the use to which they can put their learning.

> To learn, then, is to develop understandings which lead into, and grow out of, action; to discover a sense of agency that enables us, not only to define and make ourselves, but to do so by actively participating in the creation of a world in which, inescapably, we live together.
>
> (Ranson 1998, p. 20)

Kolb's work has also been a major stimulus for the development of experiential learning as a concept and method (see the discussion of experiential in Chapter 5). Thus, for example, some researchers have stressed the idea of critical reflection within Kolb's theory, emphasizing the importance of this part of the process if the greatest benefit is to be derived from the learning experience (Boud, Keogh and Walker 1985). Others have conceptualized critical reflection as a 'learning conversation': 'a form of dialogue about a learning experience in which the learner reflects on some event or activity in the past' (Candy, Harri-Augstein and Thomas 1985, p. 102). Such reflection might take place with the assistance of a teacher or facilitator, though with practice it might be carried out by the learner alone.

We may, however, recognize other views of learning. Jarvis gives five meanings for the concept:

1 any more or less permanent change in behaviour as a result of experience;
2 a relatively permanent change in behaviour which occurs as a result of practice;
3 the process whereby knowledge is created through the transformation of experience;
4 the processes of transforming experience into knowledge, skills and attitudes;
5 memorizing information

(Jarvis 1990, p. 196)

The first two of these definitions may be related to Gagné's, but distinguish between behaviour change occurring as a result of experience or of practice (the latter suggesting a more deliberate, educational or training, event). The change in behaviour is required to be more than temporary if it is to constitute learning, so as to differentiate the event from chance occurrences and changes due to the maturation of the individual concerned. The third and fourth definitions are closer to Kolb's views, with the former being an almost direct quotation from his writings. The latter definition adds skills and attitudes to knowledge as possible learning outcomes (see the section on knowledge and skill in Chapter 6). These additions make learning as explicitly relevant to training as it is to education.

The final meaning given by Jarvis for learning is another commonplace view. The two words, 'memorizing information', take the author (and probably many of his readers) straight back to schooldays. There is a frisson of terror surrounding the images which these words invoke; of a child (one's former self) desperately trying to commit more and more facts to memory in order to pass an examination. This is a long way from behaviour change, or from critically reflecting on our learning experiences and having internalized conversations with ourselves about them.

From the practitioner's point of view, there are at least three major deficiencies in most of these views of, and theories about, learning. One is the lack of consensus already referred to, so that there is no definitive guidance on the most effective way or ways of encouraging worthwhile learning. In practice, of course, it might be expected that learning and teaching methods would be varied, as appropriate, to take account of the individuals involved, the learning tasks and the circumstances in which the learning was taking place.

A second deficiency is the focus of most researchers upon the individual learner. We have to recognize, particularly when we are dealing with adults, that all learning takes place within a social context (Jarvis 1987), and involves the learner interacting with others individually, in groups, within organizations and in communities. Here, however, the work of researchers such as Lave and Wenger, who have focused on what they term 'situated learning' by novice and more experienced practitioners working together in 'communities of practice' (see also the discussion of this concept in Chapter 5), is offering fresh insights:

> There is a significant contrast between a theory of learning in which practice (in a narrow, replicative sense) is subsumed within processes of learning and one in which learning is taken to be an integral aspect of practice (in a historical, generative sense). In our view, learning is not merely situated in practice ... learning is an integral part of generative social practice in the lived-in world.
>
> (Lave and Wenger 1991, pp. 34–5)

The third problem has to do with the distance which theorizing often moves us away from the subject of the theorizing – in this case, learners and how they learn. The recognition of this problem is part of the reason for focusing, like Lave and Wenger, on what learners are doing, or say they are doing. A disadvantage of such studies, however, is that to date they have largely been confined to relatively easily accessed groups of learners, most notably university students (e.g. Marton, Dall'Alba and Beaty 1993, Prosser, Trigwell and Taylor 1994, Tynjala 1997).

For the educator, teacher, facilitator or trainer, as well as for the learner, the business of adult learning comes down to a largely rule-of-thumb or heuristic approach. In other words, if it works, do it again; if it doesn't, modify it or try another approach altogether. Hence, most textbooks for adult educators and trainers, while they give due attention to learning theory, resort to a 'cookbook' type approach when it comes to giving practical advice (see, for example, Brookfield 1986, Buckley and Caple 1990, Rogers 2001).

TEACHING

> the teacher's role is one of supporting student learning and that . . . role is best carried out by directing the students' attention to how to learn in different contexts and when faced with different learning tasks.
>
> (Elliott 1999, p. 13)

The idea of teaching may be thought of as a natural complement to those of learning and education. In the case of training, however, a different complementary term would probably be used, such as trainer or facilitator. These concepts fit together in pair bonds as tight as those of Romeo and Juliet or Cain and Abel. In order to learn, the reasoning runs, you have to be taught. However, as has already been suggested, learning may take place without the direct presence of a teacher, so the relationship is really the other way round; in order to teach, you need at least one learner. 'Teaching is a practical activity in which a "learned" person (to use an archaism) "learns" his [sic] pupils' (Oakeshott 1967, p. 157). As can be discerned from the use of the terms 'teacher' and 'pupil' in both this and the following quotation, teaching is usually thought of as taking place in a school or classroom setting:

> A teaching activity is the activity of a person, A (the teacher), the intention of which is to bring about an activity (learning) by a person, B (the pupil), the intention of which is to achieve some end-state (e.g. knowing, appreciating) whose object is X (e.g. a belief, attitude, skill).
>
> (Hirst 1974, p. 108)

For adult educators and trainers, and those who see learning as a lifelong process, such definitions may be seen as unduly restricted. There has, therefore, been an understandable reaction in the field against narrow interpretations of teaching:

> It would seem that to most people, teaching involves keeping order in the class, pouring forth facts, usually through lectures or textbooks, giving examinations, and setting grades. This stereotype is badly in need of overhauling ... The primary task of the teacher is to *permit* the student to learn, to feed his or her curiosity.
>
> (Rogers *et al.* 1983, pp. 17–18, original emphasis)

This reaction has led many working in adult education and training to reject the term 'teacher' itself, in part from a wish to distinguish themselves from schoolteachers, and in part because of the perceived inappropriateness of what are seen as typically schoolteaching methods to adults (see also the discussion of andragogy in Chapter 5). Thus, in addition to educators or trainers, we may style ourselves facilitators, tutors, lecturers, human resource developers, change agents and many other terms.

The first of these alternatives, for example, has been defined in the following fashion:

> a *facilitator* ... is a person who has the role of helping participants to learn in an experiential group ... Teaching is no longer seen as imparting and doing things to the student, but is redefined as *facilitation of self-directed learning*.
>
> (Heron 1989, pp. 11–12, original emphasis)

The use here of the terms 'experiential' and 'self-directed learning' makes the connections with the field of adult education and training clearer (see the section on experiential, problem-based, independent and self-directed in Chapter 5). It does not, of course, preclude the use of such approaches in the education of children.

Yet, whatever 'teachers' may call themselves, they remain primarily concerned with how best to encourage and develop relevant learning in their clients. As adult educators or trainers, however, the focus of attention is less likely to be on methods or models for teaching (Brady 1985, Joyce, Calhoun and Hopkins 1997, Joyce, Weil and Showers 1992), and more likely to be on learning and learning processes. More recently, these ideas have been taken up with enthusiasm in other sectors of post-compulsory education, notably higher education:

There are, however, several sets of ideas here. One is that learning rather than teaching should be regarded as the primary task in education and that there must be more emphasis on identifying how learning can best be enabled ... Closely linked to this is the idea that learners rather than teachers are central to the educational process and that needs and aspirations of students rather than the aims and values of academics should constitute the driving principle.

(Askling, Henkel and Kehm 2001, p. 345)

The main distinctions between adult forms of learning and child education may then be seen to lie in the extent to which the former involves negotiation, recognition of experience and a greater degree of partnership between learner and teacher, trainer, facilitator or whatever.

DEVELOPMENT

training, development and education are essentially concerned with learning. Furthermore, development appears to be the primary process to which training and formal education contribute.

(Garavan 1997b, pp. 41–2)

Development may be viewed as operating at a variety of levels: macro, meso and micro. At the macro-level, it has to do with nations and international relationships, while at the micro-level it is individual and personal. In between, at the meso level, it has relevance for organizations and communities. All of these levels are relevant to adult education and training, and there are fairly obvious connections between them.

There are a number of related concepts in widespread use which are almost synonyms for development. The term 'growth' is often used in a similar fashion to development, particularly at the national and individual levels. More generally, it is also very common to speak of 'change'. And, perhaps more controversially, there are ideas like progress and modernization, which more clearly embody notions of direction and betterment. All of these terms have to do, implicitly or explicitly, with the relationships and interdependencies between individuals, organizations or nations.

At the national level, development may be viewed wholly from an economic perspective, defined and measured in terms of output, and expressed quantitatively in terms of monetary units. It then has to do with how much is being produced by the individuals and organizations within the nation, with how efficient that production is, and how this is improving. Thus, we speak of more or less developed countries, systems or regions. Education and training are seen as contributing to national development by increasing the knowledge and skills of workers, and hence their output and productivity (see the discussion of work-related concepts, particularly human capital, in Chapter 4).

From this economic perspective, the notions of development and growth may be distinguished:

> Although economic development is conventionally defined in terms of a rise in real gross national product (GNP) per capita, a distinction can usefully be made between development and growth. Growth may involve no major change in factor inputs nor any transformations in existing institutions. By contrast, development presupposes a process of innovation in which new technologies will be generated and new input and output mixes will emerge.
>
> (Foster 1987, p. 93)

Those involved in development studies, however, are likely to see development as an inter-disciplinary concept, with cultural, political and social components in addition to the economic and technological ones (Hettne 1990, Preston 1996). From this broader perspective:

> development is used ... to describe the process of economic and social transformation within countries. This process often follows a well-ordered sequence and exhibits common characteristics across countries ... we can say that development has occurred when there has been an improvement in basic needs, when economic progress has contributed to a greater sense of self-esteem for the country and the individuals within it, and when material advancement has expanded the range of choice for individuals.
>
> (Thirlwall 1994, p. 9)

A clear linkage is made here between national and individual impacts. It is also being suggested, though this is by no means generally accepted (Tucker 1999), that nations tend to proceed along a common trajectory of development, with less developed countries repeating the history of developed countries as they pass through the process. The contrary argument is that it is rather more complex than that. The single trajectory model for development seems unnecessarily simplistic, given the diversity of cultures across the world. Even at the most general level, different development paths may be traced for the older and newly industrialized countries: Taiwan and Singapore are not simply repeating the experience of Britain and Germany.

The relative positions of developed and developing are also in a state of constant flux, as developed countries are themselves continuing to develop. Indeed, it is the developed countries that may be seen as effectively defining the development relationship: 'The relationship of developers and those to-be-developed is constituted by the developer's knowledge and categories' (Hobart 1993, p. 2). If these points are accepted, it becomes inadequate to see the concept simply in terms of some idea of progress, with developing countries catching up by following the historical example of developed countries. Rather, at the macro-level, development may be viewed as concerning the web of relationships, dependencies and inequalities between developed and developing countries.

When seen in personal terms, the concept has an analogous set of meanings:

> Development is the all-important primary process, through which individual and organizational growth can through time achieve its fullest potential. Education is a major contributor to that developmental process, because it directly and continuously affects the formation not only of knowledge and abilities, but also of character and of culture, aspirations and achievements. Training is the shorter-term, systematic process through which an individual is helped to master defined tasks or areas of skill and knowledge to pre-determined standards.
>
> (Harrison 1992, p. 4)

Other discussions similarly differentiate development from training (e.g. Buckley and Caple 1990). The word 'development' also appears in the term human resource development (discussed in Chapter 4), which has to do with the role of encouraging, arranging and promoting individuals' development, particularly in an organizational and employment context.

Development at the personal level need not, however, have a vocational implication or context. It may, like development at the national level, be liberal, radical or political in nature. Thus, Freire's idea of 'conscientization' (discussed in Chapter 5), formulated originally through literacy work in disadvantaged communities, may be interpreted as being primarily about individual and community development.

More generally, it is commonplace to see the roles of adult educators and trainers as being primarily concerned with the development of learners: as individuals, within groups or organizations, and within society as a whole. We may, thus, see clear linkages, in terms of development, between individual and national levels; whether these are mediated through economic or community organizations, and whether the development process emphasizes vocational, liberal or radical change.

VOCATIONAL OR LIBERAL?

The discussion in this chapter will have made clearer, if they were not already apparent to the reader, some of the tensions that exist regarding the understanding of the field of adult education and training. One of the most prevalent of these tensions is that between vocational and non-vocational or liberal interpretations of education and training. This tension is apparent in the very terms education and training, as well as within concepts like development and growth. This tension has a long history and continues to underlie a very active contemporary debate. It is also subject to the swings of fashion; so that, while the liberal view dominated European and North American discussions immediately after the Second World War, the vocational view has now been prominent for at least two decades (see also Chapter 4, which discusses work-related concepts).

These changes in emphasis have affected adult education and training at least as much as, and arguably more than, child education (Crombie and Harries-Jenkins 1983, McIlroy and Spencer 1988). Thus, in Britain, older practitioners of adult education in the universities may still hark back to the 'great tradition' of the tutorial class, associated with the names of such as Mansbridge and Tawney. In such classes, groups of earnest workers dedicated themselves to the serious, spare-time, open-ended study of 'liberal' subjects over a period of years. Little of this activity now remains, partly because of the expansion of provision, with the emphasis now on shorter courses and accreditation (see the discussion of adult and continuing in Chapter 3, and of accreditation in Chapter 7).

The terms liberal and vocational are, of course, imprecise, emotional and ideological. Just as, at the level of the individual, we may conceive of the same learning experience as being vocational for one learner but non-vocational for another (e.g. an 18-year-old and a retired person following the same degree course), so may advocates of these two apparently opposed positions label provision as it suits their cause:

> The phrase 'liberal education' has today become something of a slogan which takes on different meanings according to its immediate context. It usually labels a form of education of which the author approves, but beyond that its meaning is often negatively derived. Whatever else a liberal education is, it is *not* a vocational education, *not* an exclusively scientific education, or *not* a specialist education in any sense.
>
> (Hirst 1974, p. 30, original emphasis)

Following this view, liberal and vocational become defined in terms of each other, or, rather, in terms of distorted and partial perceptions of each other. It is rather like a two-party political system, where government and opposition alternate, and may change their policies, but remain united in their continuing rejection of each other's positions, whatever they may be at any particular time.

These differences do have real consequences, however, for the nature of the education and training opportunities made available, so it is important to try and understand what lies behind them. For one author, liberal education is characterized by the following features:

1. What should be learnt is rooted firmly within intellectual disciplines.
2. To be educated is to be initiated into these disciplines . . .
3. The point or the value of the apprenticeship into the intellectual traditions, through which we come to understand and shape our experience, requires no further justification than reference to their own intrinsic value . . .
4. That initiation is a hard and a laborious task . . .

5. The control and the direction of that conversation, and thus of the initiation into it, must lie in the hands of those who are authorities within it . . .

(Pring 1993, pp. 54–5)

The same author sees vocational education in these terms:

1. The value of the educational encounter between teacher and student lies partly in the external purposes which it serves . . .
2. Therefore, the curriculum must be planned in terms of specific objectives which arise . . . from an analysis of what the economy needs or what skills certain occupations demand . . .
3. The content of the curriculum . . . must be relevant to industry and commerce.
4. The context of learning must be, as far as possible, in a realistic economic setting.
5. The educational experience as a whole should foster attitudes and dispositions such as entrepreneurship and enterprise . . .
6. People from outside the academic and educational communities must be partners in the establishment of these objectives and in assessing whether or not they have been reached.

(ibid., p. 62)

These characterizations are supported in other recent discussions of the concepts (e.g. Barrow and Milburn 1990, Williams 1994). These kinds of lists are, however, inevitably rather stereotypical, and tend to buttress the oppositional view of liberal and vocational approaches to education. Thus, we might apply, in the former case, identifiers such as broad, general, long-term, elitist, humanist, progressive, guided by professionals and even 'useless'. Whereas, for the latter, we could come up with narrow, specific, short-term, mass market, utilitarian, immediate, guided by practitioners and 'useful'.

Yet, just as the same learning experience may serve vocational and liberal purposes, however it may be designated by the provider, so are the concerns of avowedly liberal or vocational advocates similar in many ways. One of the surprising features of the rise of vocationalism over the last decade has been the extent to which it has been accepted, and even endorsed and welcomed, by many academics and educators. While a cynical or sceptical commentator might argue that this is because they have been cowed into acceptance by their paymasters, it may also be recognized that at least some of the policy changes introduced have been useful in a more general educational sense.

Similarly, many of those involved in the delivery of explicitly vocational education or training have shown their concern to broaden the learning experience:

> workers and managers in a post-industrial economy must learn primarily not new skills but new roles. But since training ... is based on the rigid separation of the training encounter from the natural world of work, it is unsuited as a process for helping people learn new roles and develop new relationships.
> (Hirschham, Gilmore and Newell 1989, p. 185)

While the liberal/vocational distinction has real power, therefore, we should not let it blind us to other developments, distinctions and similarities.

FURTHER READING

Barrow, R and Milburn, G (1990) *A Critical Dictionary of Educational Concepts: an appraisal of selected ideas and issues in educational theory and practice*. Hemel Hempstead, Harvester Wheatsheaf, second edition.
    Contains general discussions of most of the concepts considered in this chapter, but from a primarily school-based perspective.
Campanelli, P, Channell, J, McAulay, L, Renouf, A and Thomas, R (1994) *Training: an exploration of the word and the concept with an analysis of the implications for survey design*. Sheffield, Employment Department.
    Detailed analysis of understandings of the concept, using linguistic analysis, with substantial methodological implications.
Jarvis, P (1990) *An International Dictionary of Adult and Continuing Education*. London, Routledge.
    A useful general source which includes brief analyses of many of the concepts included in this and later chapters.
Lawton, D and Gordon, P (1993) *Dictionary of Education*. Sevenoaks, Hodder and Stoughton.
    Useful for gaining a rapid introduction into many contemporary British educational issues, with a school-based emphasis.
Pring, R (1993) 'Liberal education and vocational preparation', pp. 49–78 in R Barrow and P White (eds) *Beyond Liberal Education: essays in honour of Paul Hirst*. London, Routledge.

A recent example of the English philosophy of education school of writing.

Tuijnman, A (ed.) (1996) *International Encyclopedia of Adult Education and Training*. Oxford, Pergamon, second edition.

A massive source of information on concepts, policies and provision internationally.

Chapter 2

International Concepts

THE GLOBALIZATION OF ADULT EDUCATION AND TRAINING

The three concepts discussed in this chapter – lifelong education, the learning organization and the learning society – are grouped together because they jointly illustrate the post-Second World War growth in international thinking, policy-making and transfer of ideas in the arenas of adult education and training. These developments have been reflected in the – sometimes overlapping, sometimes competitive – work of a series of international organizations. These include the United Nations Educational, Scientific and Cultural Organization (UNESCO), the Organization for Economic Cooperation and Development (OECD), the European Union (EU), the Council of Europe, the International Labour Office and the World Bank.

The key theme that can be seen to underlie the discussion throughout the chapter, therefore, is that of globalization, a process which has been affecting adult education and training at least as much as other fields. Globalization has been defined as:

> the *processes* through which sovereign national states are criss-crossed and undermined by transnational actors with varying prospects of power, orientations, identities and networks.
>
> (Beck 2000, p. 11)

> an historical process which engenders a shift in the spatial reach of networks and systems of social relations to trans-continental (or interregional) patterns of human organization, activity and the exercise of social power.
>
> (Perraton 2000, p. 128)

Globalization as an idea is much discussed at the present time. Two related aspects of this debate concern the extent to which globalization is actually happening, and whether it is being accompanied by a parallel localization and/or exclusion of sections of society (see also the discussion of social inclusion in Chapter 7). These debates can be traced throughout the examination of the concepts in this chapter.

The concepts of lifelong education and the learning society first became the subject of extensive discussion during the 1960s and 1970s, though they have earlier antecedents. There were at least three main reasons for their articulation at that time:

- the (perception of the) increasing pace of economic, social and technological change on a global scale;
- the belief that existing education and training practices and provision were inadequate to cope; and
- the conviction that educational opportunities should be available to all.

These concepts were developed against a backcloth of critical debate regarding the role of formal institutions and curricula, led by influential writers such as Freire and Illich (Freire 1972, Illich 1973).

With the hindsight that thirty or forty years provides, some of these discussions may now seem to lack practical purchase and to convey undue optimism about the possibility for democratic change based on reasoned argument and widespread participation in education and training. The associated structures of the welfare state, interventionist government and supranational organization have all come in for a good deal of criticism in the last three decades. Yet the concepts of lifelong learning and the learning society have not gone away; on the contrary, as the discussion which follows demonstrates, in the last few years they have been reborn and become the subject of increasing attention at the level of both policy and research.

The concept of the learning organization is rather more recent in origin. It came to prominence in the 1980s, offering a meso, organizational level of analysis between the macro, societal focus evident in the concept of the learning society and the more micro, individual level of lifelong education.

LIFELONG EDUCATION

The concept of LLL [lifelong learning] emerged almost simultaneously in the Council of Europe, UNESCO and OECD in the late 1960s as 'recurrent education', 'adult education' or *éducation permanente*. The central idea was the same: the development of coherent strategies to provide education and training opportunities for all individuals during their entire life.

(Jallade and Mora 2001, p. 362)

The origins of the concept have been traced back to the writings of Dewey, Lindeman and Yeaxlee in the early twentieth century (Jarvis 1995, Lengrand 1989). In essence, lifelong education and/ or lifelong learning, like the other concepts discussed in this chapter, argue for a rejection of a model of education that is confined to childhood, adolescence and early adulthood. Instead, learning is portrayed as being available throughout life, as needed and desired, for everyone.

However, having attracted a great deal of interest, particularly at international level, in the 1960s and 1970s, discussion and usage of the concept then suffered a slump, only to return with a vengeance in the mid-1990s, this time at both international and national levels:

The European Union designated 1996 'the year of lifelong learning'. The meeting of the education ministers of the Organization for Economic Cooperation and Development in January of the same year used the slogan 'Making lifelong learning a reality for all'. The 1996 report of the United Nations Educational, Scientific and Cultural Organization's International Commission on Education for the Twenty-first Century adopted 'learning throughout life' as its key concept. At their meeting in Cologne in June 1999 the members of the Group of Eight ... agreed to promote mass education throughout the world, and named 'lifelong retraining' as a priority.

(Knapper and Cropley 2000, pp. 1–2)

It seems reasonable, then, to ask why there has been this remarkable resurgence of interest in the concept. The most plausible explanation seems to be that, while the understanding of the concept and the content of the policy may vary, lifelong learning offers a useful label for policy-makers:

As a phrase, lifelong learning has in several European nations – generally with Social Democratic parties in power – become a convenient political shorthand for the modernizing of education and training systems. As in the intergovernmental agencies, it is often associated with attempts to increase competitiveness and innovation at a time of intensifying global trading pressures, by promoting investment in human resources across the life span and in a variety of settings. To this extent, it is becoming part of the accepted policy discourse of the western nations.

(Field 2001, p. 11)

The implications of lifelong education have been usefully summarized by two of its main proponents in the following fashion:

Lifelong education . . . is a set of organizational and procedural guidelines for educational practice. Its goal is lifelong learning – learning carried out throughout life. It is important to make clear at once that what is meant here by 'learning' is not the spontaneous, day-to-day learning of everyday life . . . The kind of lifelong learning that is the object of lifelong education . . . has the following four definitive characteristics:
1. It is intentional – learners are aware that they are learning.
2. It has specific goals, and is not aimed at vague generalizations such as 'developing the mind'.
3. These goals are the reason why the learning is undertaken (i.e. it is not motivated simply by factors like boredom).
4. The learner intends to retain and use what has been learnt for a considerable period of time.

(Knapper and Cropley 2000, pp. 11–12)

While this summation may seem restrictive in its view of what counts as learning (cf. the discussion in Chapter 1), three further features of the concept may be unpacked from this quotation and similar accounts (e.g. Aspin and Chapman 2000, Edwards 1997). First, lifelong education is seen as building upon and affecting all existing educational providers, including both schools and institutions of higher education (Kogan 2000). Second, it extends beyond the formal educational providers to encompass all agencies, groups and individuals involved in any kind of learning activity (see the discussion of formal, non-formal and informal education in Chapter 3). And, third, it rests on the belief that individuals are, or can become, self-directing (see Chapter 5), and that they will see the value in engaging in lifelong education.

There is, however, no 'standard' model of what a lifelong education system might look like. It is rather a slippery concept, which may be attractive to both totalitarian and liberal regimes, to both technologically developed and less developed societies (Cropley 1979), and applied to both vocational and non-vocational curricula.

> lifelong learning appears in the literature and in political discourse in a bewildering number of different guises. For instance, it is an instrument *for* change (in individuals, organizations and society) and as a buffer *against* change; it is a means of increasing economic competitiveness and of personal development; it is a social policy to combat social exclusion and to ease the re-entry of the unemployed into the labour market; it is a way of promoting the professional and social development of employees and of acquiring new knowledge through the labour process; and it is a strategy to develop the participation of citizens in social, cultural and political affairs. But there is also a sceptical version of lifelong learning which has received little attention . . . namely that it has become a form of social control.
>
> (Coffield 1999, pp. 487–8)

There are other theoretical objections to the idea of lifelong education, in addition to its lack of precision (Bagnall 1990, 2000). Some writers have noted the way in which its proponents tend to equate education with learning, making little distinction between different forms or levels (Lawson 1982). Others have argued that the concept adds little to the notion of adult education (Wain 1993: see also the discussion of adult and continuing in Chapter 3). The practical objections are just as telling. At the system level, financial and structural concerns appear paramount. It is, of course, a characteristic of conceptual development that little attention is typically given to pragmatic concerns like costs, but this ignorance in most writing about lifelong education does appear significant: 'Without real teachers, given real resources to empower students, lifelong learning will remain a slogan, a catchphrase, a substitute for real action' (Elliott 1999,

p. 26). The sheer scale and vagueness of the concept also trans-
lates into policy. Thus: 'the last two decades have witnessed a
flood of three lettered, alphabet soup initiatives connected with
lifelong learning: for example: APL, CPD, EHE, EDPs, IiP, NVQs,
OCNs and TECs' (Tight 1998a, p. 254).

Some of these ingredients have since been relabelled or
replaced. At the time of writing, the two most notable new
ingredients to this soup were the University for Industry
(UfI – frequently criticized for not being a university in the
commonly understood sense of the term) and Individual
Learning Accounts (ILAs – now discontinued because of fraud).
A glance at the, regularly updated, lifelong learning website
provided by the British Department for Education and Skills
(www.lifelonglearning.co.uk) confirms the bewildering and
changing variety of policies and projects, of all scales, which
may be marshalled together to make up a government's lifelong
learning strategy.

In a review of British government policy in this area, I aired
three main concerns:

> First, both in the policy documents themselves and in the
> translation from policy to practice, there seems to be a
> tendency to elide the broad view of lifelong learning for all
> with a narrower perspective on vocational education and
> training ... second ... [i]n listing a whole series of groups
> who tend not to participate in post-compulsory learning, the
> reports reviewed have usually identified their target groups
> for developing a learning society. The problem is, however,
> that this is typically done in a way which effectively blames
> non-participants ... and places upon them the responsibility
> for doing something about it ... My third concern is with the
> apparently compulsory aspect of the lifelong learning policies
> being articulated.
>
> (Tight 1998b, pp. 482–4)

The emphasis that these policies place on individuals, for taking
responsibility (and paying) for their lifelong learning (Coffield
1999), is perhaps their most fundamental flaw. This may work
for the well educated and the professional, who have been
successful in the educational system and can perceive additional
advantages from continued participation. It is hardly likely to
work, however, for those who left formal education early, with

little or nothing in the way of qualifications, but with bad memories and resentments, and who have been, relatively speaking, socially and economically excluded ever since (see also the discussion of social inclusion in Chapter 7).

LEARNING ORGANIZATION

The idea of the learning organization arises, like those of life-long education and learning, from global concerns about change and survival. While the articulation of the concept took place as late as the 1980s, at least three interrelated precursors for it (or pressures leading to it) may be identified.

The first of these derives from the concern of management consultants with how to encourage organizational as distinct from individual or group learning (Jones and Hendry 1994, Kim 1993). Organizational learning is seen as something greater than the sum of the elements of individual and group learning of which it is comprised (Dixon 1994). It represents, therefore, an interaction between the organization's component parts and the outside environment to the benefit of the organization as a whole. This school of thought is associated in particular with Argyris and Schön, and their work on organizational development, professionalism, theories of action and reflective practice (e.g. Argyris and Schön 1978, Schön 1988, Argyris 1992). Their writing on organizational learning is grounded within systems thinking:

> Organizational learning involves the detection and correction of error. When the error detected and corrected permits the organization to carry on its present policies or achieve its present objectives, then that error-detection-and-correction process is *single-loop* learning . . . *Double-loop* learning occurs when error is detected and corrected in ways that involve the modification of an organization's underlying norms, policies and objectives.
>
> (Argyris and Schön 1978, pp. 2–3, original emphasis)

The second line of thinking behind the learning organization has to do with the competitive necessities imposed by global economic and technological changes, the drive towards permanent and sustained innovation, and consequent concerns with quality and value for money. These issues are reflected in the writings of management gurus like Drucker, Lessem, Peters and Senge (e.g. Drucker 1995, Lessem 1993, Peters 1987, Senge 1990). This line of thinking has found expression in the ideas of total quality management and its derivative, total quality learning (see the discussion of quality in Chapter 6). It underlies a number of recent initiatives, such as the Management Charter and Investors in People (Critten 1993).

The third precursor for the current concern with the learning organization may be traced in changing industrial relations practice. Increasing numbers of companies operating in the less regulated industrialized economies, such as the United States and the United Kingdom, have sought to provide general educational and developmental opportunities for their employees (Forrester, Payne and Ward 1995). They typically offer an annual sum for each employee to spend on some kind of learning activity, in addition to enhanced in-company training and development opportunities. We may speculate upon the differing motivations of the managers and union representatives involved in agreeing such non-wage rewards: perhaps staff retention and motivation in the former case, and membership retention or expansion in the latter. But such employee development initiatives have caught the imagination, and are now frequently seen as a key component of the learning organization.

As may be judged from the discussion so far, the idea of the learning organization applies many of the same ideas as lifelong education and the learning society, but at the organizational or company, rather than the individual or societal level:

> The Learning Company is a vision of what might be possible. It is not brought about simply by training individuals; it can only happen as a result of *learning at the whole organisation* level. A Learning Company is an organization that facilitates the learning of all its members *and* continuously transforms itself.
>
> (Pedler, Burgoyne and Boydell 1991, p. 1, original emphasis; see also Burgoyne, Pedler and Boydell 1994)

That reads as a rather top–down, managerially imposed view, and raises the questions of who participates in, and who has authority over, such learning. Much the same sentiments have been expressed, however, in what may be seen as a more democratic, bottom–up fashion:

Learning organizations are characterized by total employee involvement in a process of collaboratively initiated, collaboratively conducted, collectively accountable change directed towards shared values or principles.

(Watkins and Marsick 1992, p. 118)

A third definition appears to offer elements of both of these approaches:

a learning organization is one that has a climate that accelerates individual and group learning. Learning organizations teach their employees the critical thinking process for understanding what it does and why it does it. These individuals help the organization itself to learn from mistakes as well as successes. As a result, they recognize changes in their environment and adapt effectively. Learning organizations can be seen as a group of empowered employees who generate new knowledge, products and services; network in an innovative community inside and outside the organization; and work towards a higher purpose of service and enlightenment to the larger world.

(Marquardt and Reynolds 1994, p. 22)

While that last phrase sounds just a little too altruistic, these authors, linking the idea of the learning organization to globalization, go on to identify a model for the global learning organization. They list eleven essential organizational elements for global learning: appropriate structures, a corporate learning culture, empowerment, environmental scanning, knowledge creation and transfer, quality, strategy, supportive atmosphere, teamwork and networking and vision. Despite the high demands thus placed on becoming and remaining a learning organization, many organizations have been held up as examples, or at least as aspirants. These have included, in the United Kingdom, Nabisco, Rover, Sheerness Steel and Sun Alliance (Jones and Hendry 1992); and further afield, General Electric, Honda, Samsung and Xerox (Marquardt and Reynolds 1994).

A range of 'how to' publications exist which aim to demonstrate to managers and others how they can change their organizations into learning organizations (e.g. Grundy 1994, Mayo and Lank 1994). These are relatively clear in identifying the prospective benefits to the main 'stakeholders' involved: the organization's customers, employees and shareholders. For example:

Benefits for customers include ... making available to customers products and services that meet their evolving requirements more effectively than competitors ... the rate of innovation, not just in products and services, but in process adaptability and responsiveness ... Benefits for employees include ... the ability to enhance both internal and external employability ... the opportunity for better job security ... a sense of self-respect ... Benefits for shareholders include ... differentiated human assets that have more value than those of the competition ... minimising voluntary losses of good people ... the reduction in layers of management ... the reduction of costs as continuous improvement yields continuous productivity increase ... the elimination of duplication and overlapping activity ... the ability to seize market opportunities through speed of adaptation and change ... the availability of the right people with the right skills in the right place at the right time.

(Mayo and Lank 1994, pp. 9–13)

Given such an impressive list, one might wonder why all organizations are not seeking to become learning organizations as quickly as possible. Could it be that the idea is as diaphanous and unrealizable as the ideals of lifelong learning and the learning society? Or might it be that the learning organization is just one in a long line of management buzzwords, which come off the guru conveyor belt and on to the airport bookstalls most weeks? Or perhaps it is only applicable to and by certain sorts of organizations?

While interesting as a theoretical construct ... the idea of the LO [learning organization] may be of limited value in serving as a blueprint for skills policies in the majority of UK organizations. In particular, its lack of contact with the often harsh realities of cost and time pressures and external environmental constraints raises serious problems ... it seems reasonable to argue that there is little chance of achieving any very high level of organizational learning in the following circumstances, all of which are too prominent in the UK: cost-based competition; standardized products and services; a heavy reliance on economy-of-scale advantages; low-trust relationships; hierarchical management structures; people management systems that emphasize command, control and surveillance; an underlying belief that (whatever the overt rhetoric) people are a cost or a disposable factor of production; little slack or space for creativity; and a culture of blame where mistakes (particularly those of lower-status workers) are punished.

(Keep and Rainbird 2000, p. 190)

Other criticisms that may be levelled at the idea of the learning organization are many and varied. Thus, amongst those organizations that call themselves, or have been called, learning organizations, there are substantial variations in practice and experience. This can readily be demonstrated by, for example, the differences in who is included within the ambit of the learning organization: full-time staff, permanent staff, part-timers, all grades, customers, all plants, subsidiaries? It has also been questioned whether the learning organization is about empowerment or exploitation. Is it in the business of creatively seeking the views and inputs of all its members, and giving them due credit and say in their use; or is it about squeezing as much value as possible out of each unit of production, with the resulting profits channelled in traditional ways? Any concept that can encompass such radically differing viewpoints has major problems as well as considerable potential (Coopey 1996, Garavan 1997a).

Then there is the issue – the 'bottom line' in management speak – of whether learning organizations actually do any better at their business than comparable 'non-learning' organizations. Here the evidence, as with that on general linkages between educational participation and economic productivity (see Chapter 4), is both partial and difficult to interpret (Jones 1995, Jones and Hendry 1992). In other words, the consensual nature of idealizations such as the learning organization, which can become seen as the solution to problems of organizational survival and competitiveness, can act in counter-productive ways by denying the possibility of other solutions or progressions. In the final assessment:

A close look at the learning organization literature, with its rhetoric of trust and pledges of 'win–win', when contrasted with actions actually taken by many organizations defines a significant discontinuity between what is espoused and what really happens . . . Efforts expended in learning, in being

flexible, in taking on additional responsibility and self-management go unrewarded in a contemporary capitalist economy.
(Schied *et al.* 1998, p. 288)

Most recently, the concept of the learning organization has come to be bracketed with, and to some extent supplanted by, that of knowledge management. The key difference in the latter is the added emphasis placed on the role of developing information technology (see also the discussion of changing information and communication technologies in Chapter 5, and of knowledge in Chapter 6), as the following analysis indicates:

why did knowledge come to the top of the management agenda in the 1990s . . . ? Our analysis suggests that a number of factors have come together at this time. These fall under six headings:

- wealth being demonstrably and increasingly generated from knowledge and intangible assets;
- the rediscovery that people are the locus of much organizational knowledge;
- accelerating change in markets, competition and technology, making continuous learning essential;
- the recognition that innovation is the key to competitiveness, and depends on knowledge creation and application;
- the growing importance of cross-boundary knowledge transactions;
- technology limits and potential: the limits of information systems and the potential of communications and knowledge technologies.
(Quintas 2002, p. 4)

Aside from and despite this difference in emphasis, the criticisms which may be levelled at the concept of knowledge management remain much the same as those made of the learning organization:

much about knowledge's recent rise to prominence has the appearance of faddishness and evangelism. Look in much of the management literature of the late 1990s and you could easily believe that faltering business plans need only embrace knowledge to be saved. While it's often hard to tell what this embracing involves, buying more information technology seems a key indulgence.
(Brown and Duguid 2000, p. 118)

LEARNING SOCIETY

While the learning society has only recently become the subject of considerable debate in the United Kingdom, it has a longer history in other countries that have a post-war tradition of greater educational participation. These include, for example, Canada, New Zealand, Sweden and the United States of America (Boshier *et al.* 1980, Carnegie Commission on Higher Education 1973, Commission on Post-secondary Education in Ontario 1972, Husen 1974, 1986). In those societies the advent of discussion on the learning society may be linked not just to lifelong and recurrent education, but also to the development of ideas like the post-industrial society and the information society (Bell 1973, Toffler 1970). In the United Kingdom, by contrast, the contemporary connections are as much with the issues of active citizenship and the learning polity (Hayes, Fonda and Hillman 1995, Ranson 1998).

Two recent, somewhat contrasting, British definitions of the learning society are:

> A learning society would be one in which all citizens acquire a high quality general education, appropriate vocational training and a job (or series of jobs) worthy of a human being while continuing to participate in education and training throughout their lives. A learning society would combine excellence with equity and would equip all its citizens with the knowledge, understanding and skills to ensure national economic prosperity and much more besides ... Citizens of a learning society would, by means of their continuing education and training, be able to engage in critical dialogue and action to improve the quality of life for the whole community and to ensure social integration as well as economic success.
>
> (Economic and Social Research Council (ESRC) 1994, p. 2)

> A learning society is much more than a society whose members are simply well educated ... It is a place or a society where the idea of learning infuses every tissue of its being: a place where individuals and organizations are encouraged to learn about the dynamics of where they live and how it is changing; a place that on that basis changes the way it learns whether through schools or any other institution that can help foster understanding and learning; a place in which all its

members are encouraged to learn; finally and perhaps most importantly a place that can learn to change the conditions of its learning democratically.

(Cara, Landry and Ranson 1998, pp. 1–2)

These definitions suggest both the conflictual and potentially all encompassing nature of the learning society. Thus, it may be seen as spanning both vocational concerns (the link between education and economy) and quality of life issues (the link between education and personal and social development). Some, of course, define the learning society rather more narrowly, focusing on just one of these poles of interest. As defined here, however, the concept clearly builds upon the notions of lifelong learning and the learning organization, and makes use of the underlying ideas of productivity and change (Hughes and Tight 1995).

The tensions apparent within existing discussions on the learning society have been a topic of considerable debate:

'The learning society' is an ambiguous term. It is descriptive, pointing to ... complexities and underlining the centrality of change; it is analytical, suggesting the possibility that modern society ... may be ... continuing to learn about itself and steering itself along its chosen path; it is normative, urging the need for learning to have a high profile at both the individual and the societal level; and it is ontological, making a statement about the fundamental nature of modern society and pointing to the centrality of rationality. On each interpretation ... education emerges as the key institution in modern society, but education conceived in terms broader than curricula framed by the academic community for young people.

(Barnett 1994, p. 70)

Other authors have focused on identifying the alternative interpretations that have been placed on the concept, for example:

1. The learning society as an *educated society*, committed to active citizenship, liberal democracy and equal opportunities ...
2. The learning society as a *learning market*, enabling institutions to provide services for individuals as a condition for supporting the competitiveness of the economy ...

3. The learning society as *learning networks*, in which learners adopt a learning approach to life, drawing on a wide range of resources to enable them to develop their interests and identities.

(Edwards 1995, p. 187, original emphasis)

three interpretations of the learning society: as an idealised conception of society – a futuristic ideal; as a reaction to social change – a reflexive society; and as a market phenomenon of the information society – a consumer society.

(Jarvis 1998, p. 60; see also Griffin and Brownhill 2001)

While Edwards's first and third interpretations, and Jarvis's first and second, have clear resonances with the ideals of lifelong education, it is the second interpretation, Edwards argues (and Jarvis's third), which is currently dominant. This reflects the emphasis of present policy on the perceived need, in an increasingly competitive global economy, for the effective development and availability of all human resources. Yet, at least in the definitions quoted earlier, the concern for the growth of the individual and the community still remains.

While broader visions of the learning society can be seen as an improvement on strict vocationalism, they do represent something of an unhappy and unstable compromise. As a banner under which a diversity of interests – politicians, educators, industrialists – can gather, the learning society embodies an alliance between state, professions and capital. Such an alliance seems likely to marginalize the interests of the individual in pursuing learning for their own self-fulfilment. Yet, at the same time, learning society policies seem to place undue reliance on individuals:

The main thrust of policy in both the UK and the EC is to give the pivotal role in constructing the Learning Society to the individual . . . The creation of a new form of society cannot be placed solely on the shoulders of individuals. It is a responsibility which must be shared by all the social partners – government, employers, trade unions, voluntary organizations *and* individuals.

(Coffield 1998, pp. 46, 53)

Most of the criticisms that have been levelled at both lifelong education and the learning organization can also be levelled at the learning society. To their credit, the ESRC, quoted above, went on to question the notion of the learning society:

> Some of the claims made on behalf of the learning society need to be subjected to empirical test; for example, does learning pay? does it empower and enable? does it help to equalise life chances? Will the purposes of education and training for the learning society need to encompass more than selection, socialisation, and minimal levels of literacy and numeracy in preparation for the world of work? What changes in education and training will be needed for all to participate fully in the learning society? Is there a set of values or guiding principles underpinning the notion of a learning society which need to be made explicit if a culture of education and training is to be created in the UK? What would a coherent and coordinated policy to help the UK become a learning society look like?
>
> (ESRC 1994, p. 4)

Other commentators have also pointed out the considerable disparity between the rhetoric and present reality. Though survey evidence is conflicting in the United Kingdom, it is clear that adult participation rates – whether in formal education and training or in learning more broadly conceived – do not match the rhetoric associated with the concept of the learning society (Tight 1998c). While a rather larger claim might be made for some other countries, even in these cases it is at best a partial vision of the learning society that is being achieved, with many still excluded. And when consideration is given to the embedded nature of the structural inequalities associated with access to education and training in all countries, we are left with a sense of disillusionment that a learning society in its fullest sense will ever be achieved (see also the discussion of access, participation and social inclusion in Chapter 7).

IDEALS AND FASHIONS

A number of conclusions may be drawn from the analysis in this chapter. Three of these will be briefly discussed here.

First, we may question just how different the concepts are in their meanings and applications. Even a brief engagement with some of the sources quoted in this chapter will show the reader how common it is to find the concepts linked together, or even defined in terms of each other. Thus, discussions of lifelong education or learning typically also refer to the learning society, and vice-versa. And, while debates about the learning organization may take us into a different literature, that dealing with business and management, the links between this concept and the other two are also clear.

Second, the realism of these concepts as models for national or organizational systems of provision has to be questioned. We have already argued that none of them have been achieved in practice at any level, but we might also consider whether they are, by their very nature, achievable or not. It has been argued that these concepts are both utopian in nature and have the characteristics of myths (Hughes and Tight 1995, Tight 1994). This was recognized at the time of their development by at least some of their proponents:

> reference to the concept met with many reservations, if not hostile attitudes. Some educators expressed the view that lifelong education was nothing more than a new term to designate adult education and that its use led to confusion. Others, while recognizing the rationality underlying the concept, looked upon it as Utopian, reaching far beyond the possibilities of implementation of a great number of countries.
>
> (Lengrand 1989, p. 8)

Ideals are, of course, widely used to inform and drive policy development. But, if they remain well beyond the possibility of achievement, their effectiveness may be limited.

Third, the history of these concepts appears to tell us something about changing fashions in adult education and training, as well as, on a larger scale, in political ideology. Lifelong education and the learning society have come into and out of fashion, and now are most definitely back in fashion again, although the meanings attached to the terms may have subtly changed. The learning organization, for its part, appears to have peaked in popularity and may now be being replaced by the idea of knowledge management. Clearly, we need such labels, but their changing meaning and usage is of critical importance.

FURTHER READING

Coffield, F (1999) 'Breaking the consensus: lifelong learning as social control'. *British Educational Research Journal*, 25, 4, 479–99.
Accessible and thorough critique of the concept.
Edwards, R (1997) *Changing Places? Flexibility, lifelong learning and a learning society*. London, Routledge.
Critical and challenging review of these three concepts, though not always an easy read.
Garavan, T (1997a) 'The learning organization: a review and evaluation'. *The Learning Organization*, 4, 1, 18–29.
Useful summary of thinking at the time of writing, avoiding the uncritical positions of leading exponents.
Holford, J, Jarvis, P, and Griffin, C (eds) (1998) *International Perspectives on Lifelong Learning*. London, Kogan Page.
International collection of chapters reviewing the concept and associated developments.
Ranson, S (ed.) (1998) *Inside the Learning Society*. London, Cassell.
Collection, with editorial comments, of previously published articles on the topic.

Chapter 3

Institutional Concepts

THE INSTITUTIONAL FRAMEWORK

Most countries or systems have an established institutional and legal framework that structures the ways in which adult education and training are provided. Of course, many organizations that are not designated as educational or training institutions are also involved in this provision, and the greater amount of adult learning in its broadest sense takes place outside of all such institutional arrangements. Nevertheless, it remains the case that those organizations specifically or largely dedicated to adult education and training, particularly those of higher status, have a major influence on the overall patterns of provision and practice.

This chapter examines a series of linked concepts that have to do with the labelling, nature and organization of institutions whose sole or major purpose is the delivery of adult education and training. There is, perhaps not surprisingly, a good deal of variation here in both practice and terminology from country to country, and the terms chosen for discussion in this chapter undoubtedly reflect an anglocentric bias. All of the concepts examined are, however, in widespread and current use in a number of countries, if not wholly international in scope. All have equivalents, or near equivalents, in other, non-anglophone systems.

The concepts analysed in this chapter are:

- further and higher, two terms which together can be seen to cover all formal post-compulsory educational provision, but which make a distinction in terms of its level and/or nature;

- adult and continuing, also potentially all-encompassing terms for the post-compulsory educational phase, but which have narrower interpretations as well;
- community, a concept with a wealth of meanings which extend far beyond education and training, but in this context imply some form of local, comprehensive provision, often serving all age groups;
- formal, non-formal and informal, a threefold categorization which recognizes the importance of education, training and learning outside as well as inside education and training institutions.

This group of concepts may be viewed as collectively – or in some cases, and by some interpretations, individually – covering the entirety of the post-compulsory, post-initial, post-secondary or post-school educational and training provision available within a country (see also the discussion of lifelong education and learning in Chapter 2). The extent of this provision, and the boundaries to and within it, vary from country to country and system to system.

Part of this variation is suggested by, and has to do with, the use of the related labels post-compulsory, post-initial, post-secondary and post-school to delimit, in terms of institutions as well as age groups, adult from non-adult education and training. These four expressions may be briefly defined as follows:

- post-compulsory education or training takes place after the individual has passed the minimum school leaving age (i.e. is, in some sense, 'voluntarily' involved in education or training);
- post-initial education or training takes place after the individual has finished continuous full-time education, so will begin at different ages and/or levels for different individuals;
- post-secondary education or training takes place after the completion of the secondary school phase (i.e. tertiary education or training and beyond);
- post-school education or training takes place after leaving school.

The age at which compulsory, initial, secondary or school education ends varies between different countries, and may indeed vary within countries (as it does, for example, within the United

Kingdom between England and Scotland). It will also vary quite significantly from individual to individual. Thus, in England, compulsory education currently ends at age 16; secondary education may end at any age from 16 onwards, but would not normally last beyond 19 years; school education ends at between 16 and 19 years; and initial education finishes at any age between 16 years and the mid-twenties, depending on whether the individual concerned studies for a first degree, higher degree or further qualification immediately after completing school.

Consequently, the age at which further, higher, adult or continuing education and training begins will also vary. The position is further complicated by the overlapping roles of institutions labelled compulsory, initial, secondary or school and those labelled further, higher, adult or continuing. These overlaps are made manifest in, indeed are regarded as a strength of, the field of community education, which often seeks to serve both adult and non-adult clients, and those who missed, were excluded from or 'failed' school.

Labels may also be culturally specific. In the United States, for example, 'school' has a more generic meaning, and may be applied colloquially to almost any formal educational institution, including universities and colleges; a usage which would likely cause confusion or offence in the United Kingdom. English further education colleges play a similar role to American community colleges, which are considered to be part of the higher education system there, while both would be included within the tertiary sector in Australia.

FURTHER AND HIGHER

Further education and higher education are most often distinguished in terms of the level and nature of the education offered, with higher education being typified as the more advanced and less immediately vocational of the two. Alternatively, higher education may be seen as a specialized sub-set of further education. Taken together, the two concepts may be broadly interpreted to include all post-compulsory or post-school (though not necessarily post-initial or post-secondary) education that takes place in educational institutions. Such a definition would not be precise, however, as it ignores the institutional and age group overlaps which have already been alluded to.

In England, further education may begin at the age of 16 for those who leave school then, or it may be entered at any later age or, indeed, never. Similarly, while higher education might typically begin at the age of 18, after school and/or further education, it might also be delayed, never entered or returned to.

Further education institutions, which in some ways may be seen as intermediary between school and higher education, may offer courses found elsewhere in schools and universities, with which they may then be in direct competition. They represent a potentially all-encompassing institutional form, sometimes including what would otherwise be the local school sixth form (and then called a tertiary college), and offering a range of degree programmes franchised from or validated by a university (Cantor, Roberts and Pratley 1995, Hill 1994, Smithers and Robinson 2000). Conversely, higher education institutions may provide some further education courses, and even, in some cases, offer provision which would normally be located in schools (a feature which was more common before the Second World War: see, for example, Bell and Tight 1993).

While accepting that the age at which further education and higher education begin is blurred by different national, institutional and, most especially, individual practices, we also have to recognize the varied national usage of the terms further and higher. Here, we may contrast England and Wales with the United States. In the early 1970s, the Carnegie Commission on Higher Education in the United States defined further and higher education, seen together as the components of post-secondary education, in the following terms:

> *Higher education* as oriented toward academic degrees or broad occupational certificates. It takes place on college or university campuses or through campus-substitute institutions, such as the 'open university' with its 'external degrees'.
>
> *Further education* as oriented toward more specific occupational or life skills, rather than academic degrees. It takes place in many noncampus environments – industry, trade unions, the military, proprietary vocational schools, among others.
>
> (Carnegie Commission on Higher Education 1973, p. 3)

The distinction made here is based not on age, but on the nature and institutional location of the studies undertaken. There is also an implicit suggestion of a difference in terms of level (and perhaps status) and extent of commitment. Thus, higher education may be seen as operating at a 'higher' level, demanding a lengthier period of study, and involving more abstract and theoretical learning. This distinction also embodies elements of the vocational/liberal split discussed elsewhere (see Chapter 1), with further education portrayed as the more explicitly vocational form of provision.

Yet, in institutional terms, as already suggested, the distinction in provision and roles is not that clear cut. Some universities and colleges offer, as part of their overall provision, forms of education and training that fit the Carnegie definition of further education. Similarly, some institutions other than those identified offer academic degree programmes, including, increasingly, some industrial and commercial companies (Jarvis 2001b).

In England and Wales (Scotland has a somewhat different system of educational provision), on the other hand, further and higher education have a rather different, though at root similar, meaning. Here, further education was initially defined by the 1944 Education Act, and subsequently modified and re-phrased by the 1988 Education Reform Act as:

> (a) full- and part-time education and training for persons over compulsory school age (including vocational, social, physical and recreational training); and (b) organised leisure-time occupation provided in connection with the provision of such education.
>
> (quoted in Hill 1994, p. 21)

This definition is clearly age-related, though persons over the compulsory school age might study elsewhere than in further education institutions. There is no specific mention of the level of study, so further education could be seen as encompassing higher education. In practice, however, further education and higher education institutions have long been treated (and funded) separately and differently by the British government. Interestingly, the definition makes greater reference to liberal (social, physical, recreational, leisure-time) than to vocational forms of provision.

The Further and Higher Education Act 1992, however, removed further education colleges from local government control, giving them independent corporate status:

the colleges were effectively turned into businesses run by a chief executive answerable to a board of governors. What they did was now to be determined by the marketplace. Public money which had been channelled through the local authorities was passed to the FEFC [Further Education Funding Council] which created a market of its own in 'funding units'. In addition, the colleges were to compete for income from TECs [Training and Enterprise Councils, which, together with the FEFC, have since been replaced by Learning and Skills Councils (LSCs)] (which were roughly the employers' equivalent of local authorities), from the local authorities themselves for adult and community education, from contracts and grants for specific purposes, and through the generation of fee income of various kinds.

(Smithers and Robinson 2000, p. 192)

They have since become the flagship institutions for delivering the government's lifelong learning policies (see Chapter 2 and Kennedy 1997).

Higher education (and even the more specific, and more popular, term 'university') lacks a generally accepted, legalistic definition. Nevertheless, most British discussions treat this term as if it were fairly unproblematic. Hence, many available definitions appear to be superficially straightforward; for example:

In the United Kingdom, 'higher education' is taken generally to refer to advanced courses provided mainly though not exclusively by the universities, polytechnics [now also designated as universities], colleges or institutes of higher education. 'Advanced' in this context usually means beyond A-level standard, and in fact entrance requirements are typically stated in terms of A levels.

(Squires 1987, p. 128)

As in the case of the American interpretation, here the term is linked to particular institutional forms, indeed much the same ones as selected in the United States. These definitions are, however, rather circular in nature. Higher education is that which is provided mainly by universities and similar institutions: while universities offer, either wholly or chiefly, higher education. There is nothing in either the American or British definitions quoted here which tells us what it is about higher education which makes it 'higher'; or how it differs from 'lower' or 'not-so-high' education, other than simply by following on from it.

A few authors have, however, attempted to examine the meaning of the term in more depth; for example, in terms of what higher education does:

> Higher education benefits its students and the community as a whole. For both it develops what psychologists call affect: attitudes, emotions, motivation, values and interpersonal skills based upon feelings for others. It develops cognition: knowledge, perception and thought. And it develops adaptable occupational skills by the application of cognition and affect.
>
> (Bligh, Thomas and McNay 1999, p. 7)

One author in particular has devoted a great deal of attention during the last decade to the changing contemporary nature and meaning of higher education:

> 'higher education' is essentially a matter of the development of the mind of the individual student. It is not just any kind of development that the idea points to. An educational process can be termed higher education when the student is carried on to levels of reasoning which make possible critical reflection on his or her experiences, whether consisting of propositional knowledge or of knowledge through action. These levels of reasoning and reflection are 'higher', because they enable the student to take a view (from above, as it were) of what has been learned. Simply, 'higher education' resides in the higher-order states of mind.
>
> (Barnett 1990, p. 202)

This kind of reasoning takes us further and in a different direction, breaking away from the institutional or qualification-based focus of the definitions already quoted. It also provides some guidance as to how higher education might be identified at the individual and institutional levels. Barnett goes on to equate higher education with critical thinking and the critical life:

> a higher education for a genuinely learning society – a higher education for the critical life – imposes three conditions. First, students have to be exposed to multiple discourses ... Secondly, and more controversially, the student will be

exposed to wider understandings, questionings and potential impacts of her [sic] intellectual field ... What is further required is a committed orientation on the part of the student to this form of life.

(Barnett 1997, pp. 167–9)

Such definitions are, in principle, applicable to all countries and systems; though this would, of course, rest upon a shared appreciation of what expressions like critical reflection, higher-order states, multiple discourses and a committed orientation mean.

ADULT AND CONTINUING

Both adult education and continuing education have contested – broader or narrower, traditional or modern, radical or conservative – meanings. While the latter concept is not in such wide use, and may have passed out of fashion where it is used, the former has worldwide acceptance. The term adult, in its more general and personal sense, has already, of course, been discussed in Chapter 1. Here the focus is on what is meant, particularly in an institutional sense, by adult education or adult training.

In its more 'traditional' meaning, adult education refers not just to the age and status of its clients, but also encompasses the notion of participatory learning for its own sake and not for credit. As such, adult education is as much a movement as a set of institutions. It is often closely linked with the idea of liberal education, as in the term liberal adult education (see the discussion of 'vocational or liberal?' in Chapter 1). This interpretation of adult education has also been termed the 'great tradition', the five distinguishing characteristics of which have been identified as being:

- It is committed to a particular curriculum, to the humane or liberal studies.
- Within this curriculum particular concern is shown for the social studies ... its interest is in learning ... as a means of understanding the great issues of life ...
- It demands from ... students a particular attitude – the non-vocational attitude ... and therefore examinations and awards ... are deplored.
- It combines democratic notions about equality of educational opportunity with ... assumptions about the educability of normal adults ...

- It . . . has found in small tutorial groups meeting for guided discussion over a fairly long period its most effective educational technique.

(Wiltshire 1956, pp. 88–9)

Even at the time this account was written, however, the great tradition was recognised as being in decline, and was looked back upon, with regret, as a largely pre-Second World War phenomenon. More recently, with changes in public policy and funding, the retreat away from the liberal conceptions of the great tradition has become more of a rout (Crombie and Harries-Jenkins 1983, McIlroy and Spencer 1988). Some reflections may still be seen, however, in contemporary 'radical' forms of adult education (Evans 1987, Mayo 1997, Thomas 1982, Thompson 2000, Ward and Taylor 1986), as well as in some kinds of community education (examined later in this chapter).

In its widest sense, the concept of adult education may be taken to refer to all education for adults. As such, it occupies, like further and higher education combined, the whole territory of post-compulsory provision, and may even be seen to extend beyond this to include less institutionalized forms of provision as well. For many practitioners, however, especially those from an older generation, the distinction between 'adult education', narrowly defined, and the broader context of 'education for adults' continues to have significance:

> The 'education of adults' can . . . be seen to cover all forms of education (planned learning opportunities) for those over the age of 16 (or whatever), whether the student participants are treated as adults or . . . as if they were younger learners – taught, that is, as if they were largely or completely ignorant of the subject being studied, without relevant experience, unable to be relied upon to control their own learning, having little or nothing to contribute to the learning process. 'Adult education', by contrast, consists of all those forms of education that treat the student participants as adults – capable, experienced, responsible, mature and balanced people.
>
> (Rogers 1996, p. 47)

Many would reject both the straightforward distinctions between adults and children suggested here (see the section on andragogy in Chapter 5), and the implied focus of attention on just one part of the broad field of adult education and training. Yet the concept of adult education still carries a wealth of meanings and perceptual baggage, in the United Kingdom and elsewhere, which may be seen to effectively limit its conceptual and practical usefulness:

> The term 'adult education' carries specific connotations in the United Kingdom which imply that it is specifically liberal education, and this also has a stereotype of being a middle-class, leisure time pursuit. Underlying this implication is the idea that the adult's education has been completed and, during leisure time, the adult self-indulgently improves or broadens existing knowledge, skills or hobbies . . . it is hardly surprising that adult education is regarded as marginal.
>
> (Jarvis 1995, p. 20)

This quotation makes clear a very common view of adult education as an essentially spare-time activity. This activity is engaged in for interest or amusement by individuals whose major role is not that of a learner, but that of a worker, whether paid or unpaid, to which role education makes little contribution. The marginality of adult education, though seemingly welcomed by older practitioners, remains a problem today:

> Since World War II the education of adults has neither been willing nor able to ignore its isolation from conventional education, that is, schooling. But it has accepted it, even emphasized it in its growing attempts to establish its separate identity and its claim to equal status with schooling . . . The division between education . . . and adult education constitutes a very neglected obstacle in the way of achieving lifelong learning.
>
> (Titmus 1999, pp. 346, 350)

The definition arrived at by the United Nations Educational, Scientific and Cultural Organisation (UNESCO) is, by contrast, a good example of a broader and more 'modern' conceptualization of adult education:

> The term 'adult education' denotes the entire body of organised educational processes, whatever the content, level, and method, whether formal or otherwise, whether they prolong or replace initial education in schools, colleges, and

universities, as well as in apprenticeship, whereby persons regarded as adult by the society to which they belong develop their abilities, enrich their knowledge, improve their technical or professional qualifications, or turn them in a new direction and bring about changes in their attitudes and behaviour in the two-fold perspective of full personal development and participation in balanced and independent social, economic and cultural development.

(quoted in Kidd and Titmus 1989, p. xxvii)

This definition may be compared with that given by another international body, the Organization for Economic Cooperation and Development (OECD):

Adult Education refers to any learning activity or programme deliberately designed by a providing agent to satisfy any learning need or interest that may be experienced at any stage in his or her life by a person who is over the statutory school leaving age and whose principal activity is no longer in education. Its ambit, thus, spans non-vocational, vocational, general, formal and non-formal studies as well as education with a collective social purpose.

(OECD 1977, p. 11)

Each of these definitions can be seen to encompass both training and education, vocational and non-vocational provision, study for qualifications and for its own sake, and educational provision outside expressly educational institutions as well as within. Their separate articulation can be seen as another example of the competition between such international bodies in this area (see the section on the globalization of adult education and training in Chapter 2).

The OECD definition is the broader of the two, stated in terms of learning activities rather than educational processes. While the UNESCO definition may be equated with post-initial education, the OECD's appears equivalent to post-compulsory education. The former stresses the joint purposes of national and individual development, and can be seen as relevant to developing as well as developed countries (see the discussion of development in Chapter 1). It also neatly avoids the problem of defining what it means to be an adult, by contextualizing it in terms of local societal perceptions.

The widespread use of the term continuing education developed in the United Kingdom partly in response to the perceived restrictiveness of narrower interpretations of adult education, to which it may be seen as an alternative. It is also used partly in recognition of the changing audiences and curricula within education for adults. Thus university Departments of Adult Education, or Extra-mural Studies – the equivalent of extension or external departments in other countries – have over the last two decades changed their titles to Adult and Continuing Education, or just Continuing Education (and again, more recently, to Lifelong Learning or Education). Yet, as with adult education, there are broader and more restrictive definitions of the term in use.

The articulation of a wider role for continuing education can be seen in the work of the Advisory Council for Adult and Continuing Education (ACACE) during the late 1970s and early 1980s. In their major report, the ACACE noted that:

> Our definition of continuing education is . . . a broad one. We do not think that it is useful to draw artificial boundaries between education and training, between vocational and general education, or between formal and informal systems of provision. We include systematic learning wherever it takes place: in libraries, in the work place, at home, in community groups and in educational institutions.
>
> (Advisory Council for Adult and
> Continuing Education 1982, p. 2)

This definition would include the whole of further and higher education, in addition to a great variety of provision outside educational institutions, and much that took place outside institutions altogether. It may be contrasted with the very narrow approach to the concept at one time taken by the British government, which saw continuing education – in contrast to its non-vocational view of adult education – as being confined to post-experience vocational provision for those in employment (Department of Education and Science 1980). This would place its focus on mainly short and non-award-bearing courses, designed to update those working in professional, industrial or commercial contexts.

The broader conceptualization of continuing education gained wider acceptance within the United Kingdom during the 1980s and 1990s, coming to be seen as one of the main roles of both further and higher education institutions. The usage of the term also extended to other, particularly anglophone, countries. For some, however, the term remained reactive rather than radical, lacking either the sense of tradition attached to adult education or the activist edge of community education: 'the concept appears to be a politically neutral one neither making reference or criticism of the initial education system nor implying any form of evaluation of the total contemporary educational system' (Jarvis 1995, p. 27).

Now, however, continuing education is in the process of being supplanted by the broader notion of lifelong learning, a trend which has gathered pace both nationally and internationally since the mid-1990s (see the section on lifelong in Chapter 2).

COMMUNITY

> Community education offers a place and space for the 'voice' that is a crucial part of participation and active citizenship.
>
> (Johnston 2000, p. 23)

'Community' is one of those evocative words which sounds innately appealing and worthwhile, conjuring up images of warmth, belonging and place, yet is difficult to pin down as a useful or meaningful concept (Brookfield 1983, Plant 1974). Like some of the other concepts discussed in this book (e.g. the learning society (see Chapter 2), enterprise (see Chapter 6)), it is an ideological, and thus potentially a dangerous, term:

> Community can be the warmly persuasive word to describe an existing set of relationships, or the warmly persuasive word to describe an alternative set of relationships. What is most important, perhaps, is that unlike all other terms of social organisation (state, nation, society, etc.) it seems never to be used unfavourably, and never to be given any positive opposing or distinguishing terms.
>
> (Williams 1988, p. 76, original emphasis)

A wide range of different meanings for the term 'community' has been identified. Thus, Clark identifies five main points of entry into the idea, viewing community as a human collective, as territory, as shared activities, as close-knit relationships, or as sentiment (Clark 1987). Similarly, Newman gives six common ways of interpreting the concept: community as the working class, as the quiescent poor, as the disadvantaged, as the 'whole community', as the acceptable community, and as society (Newman 1979). He concludes that:

> There is probably no single, satisfactory definition of 'community'. But we misunderstand the word grossly if we appeal to the community as any kind of incontrovertible authority, as if we assume that the community can be represented by a single cause. One of the clues to the meaning of 'community' lies in its utter *lack* of any statutory authority.
>
> (ibid., p. 209, original emphasis)

These varied interpretations have not, however, prevented the widespread use of the concept, in education and training as in other fields, in many different countries in both the developed and developing worlds (Poster and Kruger 1990, Poster and Zimmer 1992). In some countries, particularly in Latin America and Eastern Europe, the terms popular education and folk education may be used instead of, or in conjunction with, community education. In others, especially developing countries, non-formal education (see the next section) may be the preferred expression.

Naturally, these varied uses have different institutional expressions. Community colleges, for example, exist on both sides of the Atlantic, but the term is applied to different kinds of institutions. In the United States and Canada, community colleges are in the higher education sector, and offer sub-degree and degree-level study. Their nearest English equivalent would, therefore, be a further education college, outside the higher education sector (see the discussion of further and higher earlier in this chapter).

In England, community colleges are far less widespread, but generally take the form of secondary schools which offer a range of adult education and recreational provision as well (Fairbairn 1971). In Scotland, the term community education is used more generally to refer to adult education, usually offered in association with youth and other community services (Scottish Education Department 1983). The common theme shared by these different institutional forms is their concern to recruit and serve a wide range of people: a community, though not necessarily the whole community.

The use of the term for educational purposes extends far beyond these examples, and has a lengthy history:

> A survey of twentieth-century developments appears to reveal three major strands in the evolution of community education in Britain. First, the secondary school-based village/community college movement pioneered by Henry Morris in Cambridgeshire; second, the trend towards community primary schooling in some urban areas following the Plowden Report (1967) and experimentation in the Educational Priority Areas; third, innovative work in adult education and community development undertaken in some of the Home Office sponsored Community Development Projects in the late 1960s and early 1970s.
>
> (Martin 1987, p. 22)

The first of these strands relates partly to the examples just discussed, of the community college and the community school. Like many other longer-standing movements, this 'school' of community education has its saints – Henry Morris in England, Charles Mott in the United States – its literature and its advocates. 'Community education is normally understood as the process of transforming schools and colleges into educational and recreational centres for all ages' (Fletcher 1989, p. 51).

The second – in-so-far as it relates to adult education and training – and third strands identified by Martin embody the ideas of outreach and activism. Outreach is concerned with taking educational provision to where its clients are, that is outside of established educational institutions; while activism sees the educator's role as clearly political. The third strand, in particular, links to a more radical 'tradition' of adult education, which sees educators as being the servants of the disadvantaged, and adult education as being about engendering change (Hamilton 1992, Lovett, Clarke and Kilmurray 1983, Mayo 1997).

Lovett himself has identified three main approaches within this strand, all of them explicitly linked to serving the working class:

> there are three distinct 'models' of community education ... which reflect very different views about the nature of the problems facing the working class and the policies and strategies necessary to resolve them ... *Community Organisation* ... usually implies appointing outreach workers to work outside

adult education institutions in working class communities... This ... model is in fact an extension of the liberal tradition in adult education ... *Community Development* ... takes a more active attitude ... Community educators operate in local communities working on various local projects providing information, resources, advice and, when the occasion arises, research, education and training ... *Community Action* ... places greater stress on ... learning through doing. There is more emphasis on the role of conflict in the resolution of local problems and the opportunities this provides for raising consciousness amongst those involved.

(Lovett 1982, pp. i–iii, original emphasis)

Lovett's own commitment is clearly to the last of these models, which demonstrates the strongest identification with, and commitment to, working-class communities. It also recognizes that any given community is unlikely to share a homogeneous view on a given issue. Communities, in other words, are groups that are not indifferent to each other's interests, but which are likely to contain conflicting interests.

Amidst all of these types, strands and models, what, if any, common themes may be identified? Another analyst, working within the Scottish tradition, has suggested the following:

Community Education:
1. is a life-long activity;
2. ... that lays great emphasis upon the learner's active participation in learning and decision-making;
3. ... that lays great stress upon the problems and needs of people as starting points for learning ...
4. ... that can be identified as being based within identifiable communities whether these be neighbourhoods or communities of interest ...
5. ... that lays great stress upon the process of change as well as the achievement of change in itself ...
6. is education yet claims to encompass more informal and non-formal methods and contexts.

(McConnell 1982, p. 8)

This definition makes clear the links between community education and the concepts of lifelong education (see Chapter 2) and non-formal and informal education (see the following section).

Reduced to these common conditions, however, there may seem little implied by community education that is not included within adult education, or within education in general. The ideas of learner participation, starting from the problems and needs of the learner, and educating for change, are found in many contemporary approaches to learning and education (see Chapter 5). Once the idea of community itself is broadened to apply to either an area or a common interest, most of the remaining distinctions seem to vanish, and with them goes a lot of the warmth and commitment carried by the concept as well.

FORMAL, NON-FORMAL AND INFORMAL

The notions of non-formal and informal education came to prominence during the 1960s and 1970s in international discussions on education, at the same time as lifelong education first became fashionable (see Chapter 2). Yet, whereas the latter concept has to do with the extension of education and learning throughout life, the former are about recognizing the importance of education, learning and training which takes place outside recognized specialist educational institutions.

In this trilogy, 'Formal education is that provided by the education and training system set up or sponsored by the state for those express purposes' (Groombridge 1983, p. 6). The other two concepts, non-formal and informal education, were introduced with particular reference to the problems of developing countries (Coombs 1968, 1985). They are, however, also applicable to developed countries (e.g. Fordham, Poulton and Randle 1979), though in such cases they are more likely to be labelled as community education (see the previous section).

In developing countries, the formal educational system will typically only be available to, and/or used by, the minority of the adult population. In such circumstances, non-formal education, which encompasses all organized educational or training activity outside of the formal education system, may offer a cheaper and more accessible means for delivering needed learning. Non-formal education, while not constituting a parallel system, covers:

> any organised, systematic, educational activity, carried on outside the framework of the formal system, to provide selected types of learning to particular subgroups in the

population, adults as well as children. Thus defined nonformal education includes, for example, agricultural extension and farmer training programmes, adult literacy programmes, occupational skill training given outside the formal system, youth clubs with substantial educational purposes, and various community programmes of instruction in health, nutrition, family planning, cooperatives, and the like.

(Coombs and Ahmed 1974, p. 8)

A simpler definition has, however, been offered by the OECD: 'education for which none of the learners is enrolled or registered' (OECD 1977, p. 11). This stresses the location of non-formal education outside of educational institutions. There, it takes place under the auspices of organizations that do not need to adopt the more restrictive frameworks and accreditation systems of the formal sector.

The advantages of non-formal over formal education for contributing to national and personal development (see the discussion of development in Chapter 1) have been stressed:

In the context of new development strategies, non-formal education is being viewed as more relevant to the needs of the population, especially for those in the rural areas working in the traditional sector, since it attempts to focus on teaching people to improve their basic level of subsistence and their standards of nutrition and general health ... Further, since the non-formal education process usually requires the participation of its recipients in determining the nature and content of the educational programmes, these will always tend to focus on the needs and priorities of the communities.

(Fordham 1980, pp. 6–7)

Seen in these terms, non-formal education has clear linkages not just with ideas of community education, but more particularly with the practices of educators such as Freire (see the examination of conscientization in Chapter 5).

The third member of the trilogy considered in this section, informal education, may then be seen to cover all forms of learning not included in formal and non-formal education. Thus, it refers to:

The life-long process by which every individual acquires and accumulates knowledge, skills, attitudes and insights from daily experiences and exposure to the environment – at home, at work, at play: from the example and attitudes of family and friends; from travel, reading newspapers and books; or by listening to the radio or viewing films or television. Generally, informal education is unorganised, unsystematic and even unintentional at times, yet it accounts for the great bulk of any person's total lifetime learning – including that of even a highly 'schooled' person.

(Coombs and Ahmed 1974, p. 8)

Here, there are close connections to the ideas of experiential, problem-based, independent and self-directed learning (considered irf Chapter 5). Recent research in this area has focused particularly on the role of informal learning in the workplace (see Chapter 4). 'Informal learning fits very well with new forms of work organisation and new types of management, and has the potential effect of breaking the power of the formal education system' (Garrick 1998, pp. 16–17).

TENSIONS, TRADITIONS AND DICHOTOMIES

Several themes may be seen running through the analysis of institutional concepts presented in this chapter.

One theme is that of tension. Thus, there are evident tensions between the institutional expressions of concepts and the concepts themselves. The labels adult and community, to take two examples, are used differently by different institutions. There are also related tensions between institutional practices and the legal frameworks within which they operate, as exemplified in the overlaps between further and higher education.

Then there are the tensions between institutional forms and individual needs, such that particular adults may be using the same institutions at different ages and for varied reasons. All of these tensions have both spatial, in that usage varies from place to place and country to country, and temporal dimensions, in that the application of concepts has changed historically, as well.

A recognition of this variation provides a useful link to a second theme, that of 'tradition'. This word has been put in single quotation marks not to signify its status as another concept, but to suggest the need for some caution in its use. For traditions are manufactured every day, and it is frequently the case that, when we refer to certain practices as being traditional, they are not of any great historical provenance (Hobsbawm and Ranger 1983).

Both adult education and community education have been referred to in this chapter as having traditional interpretations. In these cases, both concepts do have a lengthy history, and their traditions have a basis in historical practices. The point, however, is that, in recognizing and referring back to such traditions, we are really seeking to compare current practices with an idealized version of what once was. This is, of course, a source of further tension.

A third and final theme harks back to the discussion in the introduction of this chapter, and has to do with the relations between the various institutional forms of adult education and training and those for child and youth education. These were expressed in terms of four dichotomies: compulsory/post-compulsory, initial/post-initial, secondary/post-secondary and school/post-school.

The existence of four such dichotomies is evidence enough of the problems in drawing a clear boundary between adult and non-adult education and training. Taken together, they indicate the existence of inevitable overlaps in institutional forms – most evident in England in further education colleges, in North America in community colleges. We might, therefore, conclude that any attempt to neatly delimit a field of adult education and training, the subject of this book, is doomed to failure. Or we might, more positively, argue that it is better to think in terms of an overarching concept such as lifelong education (see Chapter 2), encompassing all forms and levels of education throughout life.

FURTHER READING

Barnett, R (1990) *The Idea of Higher Education*. Buckingham, Open University Press.

> Thoughtful and carefully structured exploration of the meaning of higher education, though the language is at times rather difficult.

Jarvis, P (1995) *Adult and Continuing Education: theory and practice*. London, Routledge, second edition.

> Standard text which contains a useful chapter analysing the various concepts discussed in this chapter.

Martin, I (1987) 'Community education: towards a theoretical analysis', pp. 9–32 in G Allen, J Bastiani, I Martin, and K Richards (eds)

Community Education: an agenda for educational reform. Milton Keynes, Open University Press.
The opening analytical chapter of a book which examines the status of community education from a variety of perspectives.

Rogers, A (1996) *Teaching Adults.* Buckingham, Open University Press, second edition.
Useful text, including a chapter which looks at the varied meanings of adult education and education for adults.

Titmus, C (1999) 'Concepts and practices of education and adult education: obstacles to lifelong education and lifelong learning?' *International Journal of Lifelong Education,* 18, 5, pp. 343–54.
Thoughtful discussion of the rhetoric and reality behind these concepts.

Chapter 4

Work-related Concepts

EDUCATION AND THE ECONOMY

The concepts discussed in this chapter focus chiefly on the relationships between, on the one hand, adult education and training, and, on the other, labour market issues and economic growth. The nature of these relationships, and their strength, weakness or absence, has been at the forefront of much recent debate on educational and training policy. Most educators, employers and politicians appear to believe implicitly that education, training and learning, broadly defined, can and should make a substantial, if perhaps indirect, contribution to economic production and growth. Indeed, many commentators use this belief to underpin their arguments for a greater investment by all concerned in education and training (Layard, Mayhew and Owen 1994, National Commission on Education 1993).

The belief in a close and manageable linkage between education and the economy may be seen in operation on at least three levels; those of the individual, the organization and of the whole society:

- at the individual level, the participant in education, learning or training may regard this as a personal investment in his or her own future, during which some financial return may be expected;
- at the level of the organization, the belief takes the form of regarding expenditure on staff training and human resource development as an investment in the survival and development of the organization;
- at the level of the society, as represented through national policy, it supports the many measures that have been taken

by governments to encourage increased participation in further, higher and continuing education, and in vocational preparation, training and up-dating.

In conceptual terms, these beliefs find expression in the related notions of lifelong education, the learning organization and the learning society (discussed in Chapter 2). These concepts encapsulate the perceived need for all to engage in continuing and productive learning activities at individual, organizational and societal levels. They enjoy a broad acceptance, at least at the political and/or rhetorical levels.

It is not surprising, therefore, to find many work-related concepts in common use in the field of adult education and training. The emphasis in this chapter is on concepts that deal with the relationship between education and the economy on a more practical, rather than political, level. Four of the concepts selected for detailed discussion – human capital, human resource development, career, and professional – are, arguably, of particular prominence at this level. They allow for interpretations that emphasize the individual or the organization, and can accommodate both broader and narrower vocational perspectives.

A fifth concept, social capital, is also considered in this chapter, even though it is arguably not really a work-related concept (though it may be interpreted by some as such). Rather, this concept, which has come to prominence relatively recently, is discussed here because of its obvious link with, and contrast to, human capital.

HUMAN CAPITAL

Since its ascendancy in the 1960s, there have been three discernible phases of human capital theory's application in national educational policy. The first stressed public investment in human capital and was dominated by ambitious claims about the positive and vital link between education and economic growth ... By the mid-1980s, human capital theorists began to flex their muscles once more, this time riding on a wave of structural adjustment policies ... the contemporary version of human capital theory differs from its predecessors in three important respects: (a) it incorporates technology as a factor that mediates the relationship between human capital and productivity, (b) it integrates elements of the screening hypothesis, and (c) it advocates private over public investment in education.

(Baptiste 2001, pp. 187–9)

As Baptiste suggests, the theory or concept of human capital was developed by economists from the 1960s onwards (Becker 1993, Schultz 1961, 1971, Woodhall 1987). Put simply, this theory encapsulates 'the idea that people spend on themselves in diverse ways, not only for the sake of present enjoyments but also for the sake of future pecuniary and non-pecuniary returns' (Blaug 1992, p. 207).

The theory has applications that go far beyond the relationship between economics and education:

Many of the key insights into the knowledge-driven economy are derived from human capital theory. The basic tenets of this theory ... include the proposition that skills inhere in individuals; that they are measurable, such as in terms of the years of formal education; and that the motivation to enhance one's human capital is based on a rational calculation of individual rates of return.

(Brown and Lauder 2000, p. 226)

Distinctions may be drawn between general and specific human capital, with the former applying to 'skills and knowledge which enhances the worker's productivity, regardless of where she [sic] is employed', and the latter to 'skills which can be productively used only by the worker's current employer' (Johnes 1993, pp. 14–15). The clear implication is that the latter will be of most concern to the employer, who will tend to see it as wasteful to educate employees for potential employment elsewhere. General human capital development is seen as being chiefly the concern of the state or community, through its provision of general education and training.

At the aggregate or macro-level, it is not difficult to produce evidence to suggest a monetary linkage between education and employment. For example, 'The difference in lifetime earnings between the average American who doesn't complete high school and the average American who completes college and continues to participate in some form of adult education is roughly $631,000' (Carnevale 1992, p. 60).

The survey data on which such broad conclusions are based may also be used in a more disaggregated form. It is then possible, with certain assumptions, to make detailed calculations of the rates of return – to the individual, to the organization, or to society – of a given investment in education or training, in terms of the discounted value of the probable future earnings of those concerned (Psacharopoulos 1987). Human capital theory argues that we do routinely make such calculations, though not usually in great detail.

This notion of individual adults as rational economic decision-makers, assessing the possible returns to different personal investments in education, learning or training (and other alternative activities or investments) and then acting accordingly, has proved a very fruitful assumption for economists. It clearly does not, however, provide a complete explanation of adults' behaviour or participation in learning. Individuals do not act wholly rationally, whether judged in economic or other terms; and nor, of course, do organizations or governments. These realizations have led economists to develop alternative or supplementary theories to accompany or replace human capital theory (Chapman 1993). Two of these developments have been particularly influential.

First, what is called the screening hypothesis suggests that what employers look for in recruits, or candidates for promotion, is not simply their human capital. They do typically look for a certain level of education or training, usually measured by educational or professional qualifications. They may be satisfied with this alone – using qualifications as a 'signal' of the needed ability – but will frequently also want other qualities or skills in addition. Possible candidates are, therefore, screened for their educational qualifications, and those who pass this initial sifting exercise may either be employed directly or proceed to a second stage in the selection process. The implication of this view for the individual is that personal investment in education is only worthwhile up to the level required to enable them to successfully pass through the screening process for the job or career they are seeking. Beyond that, they would be better advised to invest in other things.

However, it is argued that 'the weight of evidence suggests that signalling and screening account for only a small part of the differential between the earnings of relatively educated and less educated individuals' (Johnes 1993, p. 20). So it would seem that many employers do not screen, or at least not in the rigorous fashion implied.

The second, and related, theory is that of credentialism. This suggests that, in an increasingly competitive labour market, those seeking employment or promotion will need to offer more and more qualifications if they are to stand out. The number, level and standard of qualifications required for a given post is seen as rising, regardless of their relevance (Dore 1976). The implication for individuals is that they will need to invest more and more in their own education, training and development to keep up with, or stay ahead of, competing individuals:

> When students invest in their own 'human capital', as well as purchasing education in the form of a positional good they are often purchasing *savoir* [i.e. self-transformation]. In the process of (as they hope) securing access to the labour markets, they are also turning themselves into more skilful and economically competent individuals.
>
> (Marginson 1995, p. 22)

In such a climate, most if not all investments are likely to be worthwhile.

Despite these modifications to the theory, however, human capital has been subject to much critique. Writing ten years ago, Blaug (1992) saw no prospects for the further development of the theory. More recently, Coffield has provided a thorough deconstruction of the theory and its use as a foundation of policy, identifying ten key problems:

1 *The thesis is diversionary* . . . it diverted attention away from structural failures and injustices and blamed victims for their poverty . . .

2 *It overshadows social capital,* and other forms of capital (e.g. cultural, material) . . .

3 *The empirical basis of the theory is highly disputable* . . . personal characteristics and job conditions are more important determinants of work performance than educational attainments.

4 *The theory is seriously incomplete* . . . for education to be effective, it is crucially dependent on complementary inputs . . .

5 *It is dangerous* . . . The overconcentration on one factor – improving standards in education – distorts both industrial and educational policy in ways that are unlikely to improve competitiveness and delays the advent of more comprehensive strategies.

6 *It ignores polarisation* . . .

7 *It ignores the sexual division of labour* . . . skills are not neutral, technically defined categories but are socially constructed . . .

8 *It has created a new moral economy*, where some people are seen as more 'desirable' than others . . .

9 *Other options may be more appropriate* . . . instead of upskilling their workforce, companies have a range of competitive strategies to choose from . . .

10 *Upskilling creates credential inflation* . . .

(Coffield 1999, pp. 482–5)

Yet, in spite of these criticisms, belief in human capital theory continues to underpin contemporary educational and economic policies, with inevitable consequences: 'the working assumptions of policy-makers in the UK for a decade or more appear to have been derived from human capital theory . . . since they take no account of the real orientations people have to ET [education and training] they are doomed to fail' (Fevre, Rees and Gorard 1999, p. 136).

HUMAN RESOURCE DEVELOPMENT

Contemporary HRD knowledge frameworks are unashamedly linked to market economics. It is the market discourse of market economics which gives the cues to the sub-discourses of HRD practices: consultancies, re-engineering, downsizing, outsourcing negotiations and image making on the one hand, and discourses of quality performance on the other – capability, competence, total quality management, empowerment, self-direction, learning organisations, and so on.

(Garrick 1998, p. 5)

In its dominant, western interpretation, human resource development refers to a range of responsibilities and activities that have in the past tended to be located under headings such as 'personnel', 'staff development' or 'training'. It may also be seen as a more modern alternative to the notion of manpower planning, which now has a rather dated and sexist feel (Romiszowski 1990). In some other countries, however, as in East Asia, human resource development has a meaning closely analogous to that of development (discussed in Chapter 1). In such societies, the state is seen as having the core role in directing, focusing and coordinating policy and provision, rather than the individual firm or organization (Cummings 1995).

In its western interpretation, human resource development suggests a wide-ranging concern with the overall development of the individual, normally in their capacity as an employee or worker, and forms one aspect of the broader field of human resource management or planning (Harrison 2000, Megginson, Joy-Matthews and Banfield 1993, Stewart and McGoldrick 1996, Thomson and Mabey 1994, Wilson 1999). As in the case of many of the concepts discussed in this book, there is a range of definitions available:

> It should be no surprise . . . that because different disciplines lay claim to the field and emphasize different roles, each asserts a different definition of the field of practice. Each definition also implies an underlying philosophical stance regarding the nature of learning and instruction. Six characterizations capture the differing foci of these discipline-based definitions: human resource developer as competent performer, developer of human capital, toolmaker, adult educator, researcher/evaluator, and leader/change agent.
>
> (Watkins 1991, p. 242)

> While there have been many efforts to define human resource development, no consensus has emerged. In fact, there is disagreement among the field's leaders about whether or not a single definition is even a worthy goal.
>
> (McLean and McLean 2001, p. 313)

Despite their reservations, however, both Watkins and the McLeans offer their own definitions:

> the field of study and practice responsible for the fostering of a long-term, work-related learning capacity at the individual, group and organizational level of organizations. As such, it includes – but is not limited to – training, career development and organizational development.
>
> (Watkins 1991, p. 253)

Human resource development is any process or activity that, either initially or over the long term, has the potential to develop adults' work-based knowledge, expertise, productivity and satisfaction, whether for personal or group/team gain, or for the benefit of an organization, community, nation or, ultimately, the whole of humanity.

(McLean and McLean 2001, p. 322)

Both of these definitions make clear the instrumental nature of the field, focusing on work-related learning of immediate or long-term benefit. While Watkins restricts her concern to the organization, the McLeans recognize the possibility of taking a national or even international perspective. As these definitions suggest, human resource development is closely related to several other concepts discussed in this book, including career (which is also examined in this chapter), training (see Chapter 1) and the learning organization (see Chapter 2). Learning organizations, if they merit the term, should see human resource development as a central and essential aspect of their activities.

These definitions do, however, leave somewhat unclear the question of what human resource development (HRD) actually consists of, or just what it is that human resource developers do. Other authors offer plentiful guidance:

HRD as a concept, model, approach, discourse or set of practices remains unclear. A number of dimensions do, however, emerge from an analysis of the literature, specifically:

- HRD is intrinsically related to overall business strategy and competitive advantage.
- HRD is conceptualized as an investment in human resources capability rather than an employment cost.
- HRD is concerned with change at all levels, both organizational and personal.
- HRD views the employee in a 'holistic' sense.
- HRD is concerned with identifying and enhancing the core competencies required at each level to meet its present and future objectives.
- HRD focuses on the management and delivery of training activities within the organization.
- HRD concerns itself with selecting the best delivery systems designed to enhance human resource competencies.
- HRD is concerned with organizational and individual learning.

- HRD consists of a set of generic activities associated with learning.
- HRD is a social and discursive construct.
- HRD is concerned with how well human resource development strategies are reinforced by and reinforce other HR strategies.

(Garavan, Heraty and Barnicle 1999, p. 169)

Human resource development may be seen then, as the opening quote by Garrick also suggests, as a necessary, central and integrated response to a variety of contemporary pressures felt by organizations. These include competitive restructuring, decentralization, globalization (see Chapter 2), organizational acquisitions and mergers, quality (see Chapter 6) and technological changes.

There are, of course, objections to and criticisms of the idea of human resource development, and these can be found at both the conceptual and practical levels. In the former case, there are those who object to the idea of considering people as 'human resources', alongside and to some extent substitutable with non-human resources. This can seem to be both reductionist and demeaning, suggesting that individuals are only to be considered in terms of their current and prospective future economic productivity. The idea of human resource development does, though, appear to represent an advance in these terms on the notion of manpower planning, in being somewhat less directive and more individualized. Perhaps we should talk instead, of 'developing resourceful humans' (Burton 1992)?

The practical objections to the concept are similar to those levelled at the ideas of human capital and the learning organization. Namely, just how many organizations or employers are currently using human resource development in anything like the central, integrated and comprehensive fashion suggested by the textbooks? While the pressures identified by Garavan, Garrick and others are undeniably potent, in the absence of strategies based on human resource development most organizations continue to respond in a piecemeal fashion.

CAREER

In many ways career development and management succession planning are at the core of human resource development.

(Thomson and Mabey 1994, p. 122)

Seen as a human resource development role, career management and development would likely involve the application of a range of techniques. These could include, for example, career and performance reviews or appraisals, coaching and mentoring, the use of psychometric and self-assessment tests, developmental assessment centres and career planning workshops, and the provision of information on alternative career paths (Mabey and Iles 1994). Yet this is to suggest a rather narrow view of the meaning of career and career development; one which is, to some extent, supported by the inclusion of career in a chapter on work-related concepts.

Many researchers have viewed careers essentially in terms of paid employment (e.g. Arnold 1997, Arthur, Inkson and Pringle 1999). Others, however, have taken a broader perspective, seeing careers as encompassing unpaid forms of work as well as overall life choices and circumstances (e.g. Hewitt 1993, Kerckhoff 1993). The following is a well-considered example of the former approach to the study of individual or organizational careers:

> The term 'career' can mean a number of things. It can imply advancement – persons move 'up' in their career rather than 'down', although we refer to 'career moves', which may also be lateral. We also refer to people 'having a career in' some form of profession, such as medicine, banking or management, and there is an implication, if now largely out-of-date, that a career is likely to be stable over time. In fact it is becoming more common for people to think in terms of 'career port-folios', interrelated sets of work experiences that may be combined to provide career evidence for a range of jobs. Because of this, we shall define career as 'the pattern of work-related experiences that span the course of a person's life'. This defin-ition not only broadens the concept of 'career', but makes it as relevant to unskilled and manual operators as to engineers and professors.
>
> (Thomson and Mabey 1994, p. 123)

This definition usefully brings out the class associations of the term. For some, however, its supposed breadth would be by no means broad enough:

> By career I mean that trajectory through life which each person undergoes, the activities he or she engages in to satisfy physical

needs and wants and the even more important social needs and wants. The career, then, is activated in the service of both the physical being and the symbolic self.

(Goldschmidt 1990, p. 107)

The first of these definitions can be characterized as narrower and vocational. It also focuses, at least implicitly, mainly on the experiences of men, given the emphasis on paid employment and continuity. The second definition, by contrast, is much wider. It extends the notion of career both internally, in terms of its meaning for the individual concerned, and externally, linking work to the rest of life. As a concept, the latter is relevant to all, men and women, those in paid employment and those who are not.

Some, particularly older, studies of individuals' work careers have suggested that career development follows a regular pattern:

career satisfaction follows a cyclical curve. It starts at a high level (upon occupational entry), dips to its nadir ... when initial expectations of rapid advancement are delayed or thwarted, and then recovers, although not to the previous high level ... at about age 40. In contrast, career success begins at a low ebb and increases linearly from occupational entry to midlife, when an incipient decline sets in.

(Cytrynbaum and Crites 1989, pp. 68–9)

Such a view accords with many of the commonplace metaphors for work careers: the ladder, the set of steps, or the upward curve; followed by an inevitable but hopefully gentle slipping away in later life. Yet this pattern, though it undoubtedly has existed, and continues to exist, is by no means general and is rather simplified. It ignores the experiences of the many women who have 'career breaks', or who work in jobs with no development prospects, and is much less relevant in general at a time of recession and economic change. Hence, we may opt to speak instead of career patterns, paths or lines (Kerckhoff 1993).

These criticisms are confirmed by research which has focused on particular professions or areas of employment, such as teaching (Goodson and Hargeaves 1996), medicine (Allen 1994) and management (Nicholson and West 1988). These studies have provided more comprehensive understandings of patterns of career development, and have challenged the more simplistic and uni-directional views of careers:

> Organisations are not pyramids, they are scattered encampments on a wide terrain of hills and valleys, and careers are not ladders, but stories about journeys and routes through and between these encampments ... Careers, as stories of these journeys, often get better with the telling ... They provide cognitive structures on to which our social identities can be anchored.
>
> (Nicholson and West 1988, p. 94)

Studies of women's careers have contributed considerably to our understanding of the varied and broader patterns which careers may take. These studies have, naturally, paid particular attention to the often conflicting demands of home, family and work (Evetts 1994, 1996, Halford, Savage and Witz 1997, Hughes 2002, Marshall 1995). Mothers who seek to pursue or continue a work career necessarily have to make considerable compromises. They may have little alternative but to choose part-time or temporary employment. Their options are reinforced by processes of labour market segregation or segmentation, which effectively label work as women's or men's, and reserve certain types and levels of occupation, with poorer pay and conditions, largely or exclusively for women (Rees 1992, Spencer and Taylor 1994).

A further challenge to the conventional view of the career has come from recent studies of the impact of changing economic and social conditions. For those starting careers, it is clear that the transition from initial full-time education to work has become problematic, and is likely to be smooth for only a minority of entrants (Banks *et al.* 1992). Recession, automation and changing employment patterns have led to increased youth and graduate unemployment, and to increases in part-time and short-term work: 'the traditional form of work, based on full-time employment, clear-cut occupational assignments, and a career pattern over the lifecycle is being slowly but surely eroded away (Castells 1996, p. 268).

For those in work, organizational restructuring has considerably affected career expectations: 'The survivors of restructuring efforts are ... well aware that while they may still have a *job*, they may no longer have a *career* – at least in the traditional ladder sense' (Kanter 1989, p. 308, original emphasis). In these shifting circumstances, professional careers are becoming less hierarchical but more entrepreneurial, and the talk is of career portfolios or flexible careers (Arthur *et al.* 1999, Newell 2000, Pollert 1991: cf. the discussion of flexible learning in Chapter 5).

PROFESSIONAL

As in the case of the career, the linked ideas of 'profession' and 'professional' also have class and gender connotations. Unlike career and the other concepts discussed in this chapter, however, the term professional is not applicable to every individual adult, but is restricted to particular kinds of careers. It suggests both a certain, higher level of occupational activity, and a degree of exclusivity. Like so many of the terms analysed in this book, profession presents problems of definition:

> *Profession* is an essentially contested concept. Despite its widespread use in the media and in the everyday discourse of those who would be readily regarded as professional people, and despite the best efforts of sociologists, philosophers and historians, it defies common agreement as to its meaning. Professions are more easily instanced than defined, and dictionaries tend to convey the meaning of the term more through example than by identifying distinctive qualities. Where qualities are cited these usually refer to *knowledge* and *responsibility*.
> (Hoyle and John 1995, p. 1, original emphasis: see the discussion of knowledge in Chapter 6)

'Classic' professions such as medicine and law would likely be accepted as such by everybody. In most other cases, however – for example, accountancy, nursing, pharmacy, social work and school teaching – there would probably be disagreements as to status (Becher 1999). In such circumstances, it may be best to treat professionalism as an essentially ideological notion (Eraut 1994).

A variety of approaches have, nevertheless, been developed to summarize the characteristics and enable the identification of professions. These include the use of typical traits or sets of criteria, divisions of labour and occupational control (Jones and Joss 1995). Different forms of profession may be recognized, such as the practical, technical and managerial. They may also be distinguished in terms of their self-image, theoretical orientation, knowledge and value base, practice theory and client relations.

Similarly, distinctions may be identified in the ways professionals are educated or trained. Bines and Watson have identified three successive models of professional education:

> The first can be characterised as the 'apprenticeship' or 'pre-technocratic' model. Professional education takes place largely on the job ... The curriculum largely comprises the acquisition of 'cookbook' knowledge embodied in practice manuals and the mastery of practical routines. Instruction is largely provided by experienced practitioners ... The second model, called here the 'technocratic' model, has become the pattern of professional education for a large number of professions in recent years. It has tended to take place in schools associated with, or incorporated in, institutions of higher education. It is characterised by the division of professional education into three main elements ... the development and transmission of a systematic knowledge base ... the interpretation and application of the knowledge base to practice ... supervised practice in selected placements.
>
> (Bines and Watson 1992, pp. 14–15)

The third model identified, the 'post-technocratic', is seen as still being in the process of development. It emphasizes the acquisition of professional competencies through practice and reflection, with students having skilled practitioners as coaches or mentors. It may also be characterized by the increasing emphasis placed upon continuing professional development (Clyne 1995), accepting that professionals, like all workers, can no longer expect to be prepared for their whole careers during their initial education.

SOCIAL CAPITAL

Though the concept of human capital (discussed earlier in this chapter) has been widely critiqued, it has remained highly influential in national and international policy-making on education and the economy. The last decade has witnessed the rise to prominence, in both policy-making and academic circles, of the somewhat complementary concept of social capital. Its acceptance and application may be seen as both a recognition of the flaws in the concept of human capital and as an attempt to extend its impact beyond the workplace and into the community.

The meaning and application of the term has been explained in the following terms by two of its key proponents:

> Social capital is the aggregate of the actual or potential resources which are linked to the possession of a durable network of more or less institutionalised relationships of mutual acquaintance and recognition – or, in other words, to membership of a group – which provides each of its members with the backing of a collectively-owned capital.
>
> (Bourdieu 1997, p. 51)

> Social capital . . . refers to features of social organization, such as trust, norms and networks, that can improve the efficiency of society by facilitating coordinated actions.
>
> (Putnam 1993, p. 167)

Other forms of capital have also been recognized alongside social capital, human capital and physical capital (i.e. resources which have a readily tradeable monetary value). These include cultural and intellectual capital, which, like human capital, are seen as vested in individuals. 'Unlike other forms of capital, social capital inheres in the structure of relations between persons and among persons. It is lodged neither in individuals nor in physical implements of production' (Coleman 1990, p. 302).

Not surprisingly, the relationship between human and social capital has been the subject of much analysis:

> The key distinction between human and social capital is that the former focuses on individual agents, and the latter on relationships between them and the networks they form . . . Human capital is measured primarily by levels of qualification achieved . . . Social capital is . . . measured broadly . . . in terms of attitudes or values, or by levels of active participation in civic life or other networks . . . Human capital suggests a direct linear model: investment is made, in time or money, and economic returns follow . . . Social capital has a much less linear approach, and its returns are less easily definable.
>
> (Schuller 2001, pp. 20–1)

Human and social capital are not in direct opposition to each other, but in a relationship of tension, theoretically and pragmatically.

> (Field, Schuller and Baron 2000, pp. 250–1)

Social capital, in short, has to do with networks and trust, and the support that these provide to individuals and groups within society. These factors are now seen as being of key importance in societies, such as many of those in the western world, which have moved away from more 'traditional' forms of family and community organization, and are experiencing both growing individualism and increasing globalization.

Some authors, however, have detected conceptual confusion in the ways in which the term is used:

> For the most part it is used to refer to norms, values and networks associated with traditional family and community linkages which are being undermined by globalisation and associated socio-economic forces, necessitating their urgent rational reconstruction in a range of social spheres . . . At other times, the concept is used to refer to a new set of identities, networks, and values associated with social movements or democratic forms of institutional/civic engagement. Whatever it defines, in all these analyses social capital is used in such a way as to place the main emphasis upon social cohesion.
>
> (McClenaghan 2000, p. 580)

Other criticisms have focused upon the ways in which the concept of social capital has been seized upon and applied by politicians:

> The fundamental concern with the way the term 'social capital' has been converted into political currency is that it is being used to rationalize cheap remedies for problems which require new ways of thinking and considerable redistribution of income.
>
> (Brown and Lauder 2000, p. 228)

By contrast, a fuller analysis of the implications of the idea suggests that policies that seek to develop it will have to be much more comprehensive and far-reaching:

> In order to promote extensive social capital for rising gener-ations, government will have to redefine the relationship between public and private, in the light of the importance of coproduction – partnership – and investment in widespread citizen participation. This means, first, more transparency in central government activities and the use of public resources.

Second, much more authority and power will need to be devolved to properly open and participatory organs of local government to enable them to energize local economies and clusters of companies by being sensitive and responsive to the requirements and needs of citizens, businesses, and the full range of civic associations in their local contexts.

(Szreter 2000, pp. 76–7)

Recovering or redeveloping social capital lost through the rise of capitalism, but now seen as essential for competitive survival in a world of global capitalism, is clearly, then, not going to be a straightforward or short-term process.

However, the most damning critique of the concept is not to do with its meaning, application or practicality, but rather with its use as a substitute for the harder-edged and rather discredited term human capital, and the extent to which it replicates the same kinds of faults (see Blaxter and Hughes 2000). From this perspective, both human and social capital see the individual as a rational, economic decision-maker, taking whatever course is in their best interests in financial terms in any given set of circumstances, whether at the individual, family, group, organizational or societal level (hence, social capital may also be seen at one level as a work-related concept). Yet, such a perspective, while understandably persuasive to politicians and academics alike, massively underplays the complexity of human motivations and decision-making processes.

LINKAGES AND INTERCONNECTIONS

The five concepts discussed in this chapter have obvious interconnections. Thus, human resource development may be viewed as the process or processes by which human (and possibly social) capital is developed. Similarly, the career and its advancement can be seen as one of the key concerns of the human resource developer, and might also be thought of in terms of the application of individual human capital throughout the lifespan. Professions constitute a particular kind of career, and the role of human resource developer could itself be termed a profession. Human and social capital, despite or perhaps because of the arguments of their proponents, appear indelibly linked.

These concepts do have a clearly work-related context, as do a number of others considered elsewhere in this book (see, for example, the sections on the learning organization in Chapter 2, and on skill, competence and quality in Chapter 6). However, they can also be interpreted more generally. This is particularly so in the case of career, where it has been argued that it is more useful to see the term as relating to the whole life rather than to just that component of it concerned with paid employment; and of social capital, which seeks to recognize and analyse the different kinds of capital built up by individuals in all aspects of their lives.

Taking this perspective, and interpreting the concepts discussed here as operating primarily in practical rather than political terms, we can also view them as providing useful linkages between the levels of individual, organization and society. Each of the concepts examined has individual and organizational elements, and each needs to be seen in the wider context of society as a whole. They deal with the development, productivity and output of individual adults as they impact upon the adults themselves, upon their employers or organizations, and upon the communities and nations of which they are a contributing part.

FURTHER READING

Arnold, J (1997) *Managing Careers into the 21st Century*. London, Paul Chapman.
  Accessible analysis of the current and changing nature of work careers.
Baron, S, Field, J and Schuller, T (eds) (2000) *Social Capital: critical perspectives*. Oxford, Oxford University Press.
  Up-to-date discussion of the development and application of the concept.
Blaug, M (1992) *The Methodology of Economics: or how economists explain*. Cambridge, Cambridge University Press, second edition.
  Accessible discussion of a wide range of economic theories, including human capital theory.
Eraut, M (1994) *Developing Professional Knowledge and Competence*. London, Falmer Press.
  Focuses on the nature of professional knowledge, its development and assessment.
Harrison, R (2000) *Employee Development*. London, Chartered Institute of Personnel and Development.
  Standard how-to-do-it textbook including material on human resource development, career development and the learning organization.

Johnes, G (1993) *The Economics of Education.* London, Macmillan.
General introduction to economic perspectives on education, including human capital theory and rate of return analysis.

Wilson, J (ed.) (1999) *Human Resource Development: learning and training for individuals and organizations.* London, Kogan Page.
Twenty four chapters cover different aspects of learning, training and development in organizations.

Chapter 5

Learning Concepts

THE ORGANIZATION AND PRACTICE OF ADULT LEARNING

This chapter considers a series of related concepts that are concerned with the methods by which adult education, training or learning are practised and organized. There are a plethora of such concepts, and new ones seem to be created (or re-created) every time a supposedly innovative learning initiative is launched.

For convenience, these 'learning' concepts can be divided into two main groups:

- those which focus mainly on the perspective of the organization providing education or training; and
- those which are more concerned with the perspective of the individual learner.

It has to be recognized, of course, that this division is rather artificial, and that there are overlaps between the two groups.

The first group of concepts, emphasizing the organizational perspective, can be seen to include terms such as distance, flexible and open learning or education. There are, in addition, many other related, synonymous, cognate or precursor concepts – such as correspondence, external and non-traditional provision – which belong with this group and merit some consideration.

The second group, stressing the individual learner's perspective, includes the closely linked concepts of experiential, problem-based, independent and self-directed learning. Once again, there are a series of related terms that need to be borne in mind, including action, discovery, learner-managed and student-centred learning.

Two of the most widely discussed terms in adult education, andragogy and conscientization – ideas which have claims to be considered as the most, or perhaps only, original theories to be developed by adult educators – also belong in the second, individual group of learning concepts. They will be discussed separately, however, in recognition of their history and status. A third, more recently articulated concept – communities of practice – which also has links with the work-related concepts discussed in Chapter 4, will be examined alongside them.

What all of these concepts share in common, through their focus on the organization and practice of adult education and training, is a concern with issues of control and responsibility. Put simply, the concepts in the organizational group have to do with the ways in which those who provide education or training choose to offer these opportunities, with the control over the nature of this provision essentially retained by the institutions concerned. In the case of the concepts included in the individual group, however, something of a shift of responsibility from the institution to the individual may be observed, with control over learning resting to a larger, though by no means absolute, extent with the individual learner.

The chapter concludes with a discussion of changing information and communication technologies, both to illustrate and critique the pace of conceptual development in this area.

DISTANCE, OPEN AND FLEXIBLE

As suggested in the introduction, the three concepts on which this section will focus – distance, open and flexible learning, education or training – are selected, though arguably central or at least representative, examples from a wider group. This broader group includes other terms which are precursors of, related to, or synonyms for, the three concepts chosen for more detailed exploration.

Thus, correspondence and external study may be seen as precursors of distance education, to be distinguished from it largely by the range and level of educational technologies used (Glatter et al. 1971, Houle 1974). Some now recognize a third 'generation' of practice in this area, developed from distance education and characterized by the use of computer-based instruction (Mason and Kaye 1989), to which, more recently, the term distributed learning has been applied (Lea and Nicoll 2002, Rumble 2001). This theme is further considered in the final section of this chapter. As a concept, distance education has itself now been partly superseded by the term open learning. However, the latter, like flexible learning, has a broader meaning as well, and could be seen as encompassing all of the concepts included in this chapter.

The organizational group of concepts can also be seen to include overlapping, but narrower or less universal, terms such as extra-mural, non-traditional and part-time. There are also links between this group and ideas such as access and modularization, which are considered with other 'structural' concepts in Chapter 7. The boundaries between conceptual groupings such as these are, evidently, difficult to draw, and the particular relationships discussed here should not be seen as hard and fast.

These problems of association may be further illustrated with reference to the terms programmed and discovery learning, both of which might have been considered in some detail in this chapter, but were judged to be of lesser significance. Thus, programmed learning now seems a dated and directive concept, yet was once thought by some to hold great promise. Discovery learning, on the other hand, sounds a relatively timeless and idealistic notion. Yet both terms can be linked to generally desirable sounding ideas like open, flexible, independent and self-directed, and to each other, through the concepts of distance education and experiential learning.

Distance

The last two decades have witnessed an international upsurge of research in distance education, largely stimulated by the creation of the British Open University (Perry 1976) and of similar institutions in other countries. This research has included both comparative analyses of alternative systems (e.g. Harry 1999, Kaye and Rumble 1991) and theoretical developments (e.g. Evans and Nation 1992, Perraton 1987). A series of authors have attempted to define distance education and suggest areas for further study within this field.

Thus, Holmberg built on the notion of distance education as a guided didactic conversation:

> Distance education comprises one-way traffic by means of printed, broadcast and/or recorded presentations of learning matter and two-way traffic between students and their supporting organization. The one-way presentation of learning matter occurs either through self-contained courses or through study guides to prescribed or recommended reading. Most of the two-way traffic usually occurs in writing, on the telephone or by other media and, usually only secondarily or as a supplement, face to face.
>
> (Holmberg 1986, p. 2; cf. Holmberg 1997)

This seems to be a very precise definition, but it is also restrictive, appearing to be based firmly on the contemporary practices of a limited number of organizations, including the British Open University and similar specialist institutions in other countries.

Keegan, on the other hand, starts his analysis from an explicit recognition of the range of different concepts and practices that have been drawn together under the banner of distance education:

> 'Distance education' is a generic term that includes the range of teaching/learning strategies referred to as 'correspondence education' or 'correspondence study' at further education level in the United Kingdom; as 'home study' at further education level and 'independent study' at higher educational level in the United States; as 'external studies' in Australia; and as 'distance teaching' or 'teaching at a distance' by the Open University of the United Kingdom. In French it is referred to as 'télé-enseignement'; 'Fernstudium/Fernunterricht' in German; 'educación a distancia' in Spanish and 'teleducacâo' in Portuguese.
>
> (Keegan 1986, p. 31)

He then defines distance education in terms of five characteristics:

- The quasi-permanent separation of teacher and learner throughout the length of the learning process; this distinguishes it from face-to-face education.
- The influence of an educational organisation both in the planning and preparation of learning materials and in the provision of student support services; this distinguishes it from private study and teach-yourself programmes.
- The use of technical media; print, audio, video or computer, to unite teacher and learner and carry the content of the course.

- The provision of two-way communication so that the student may benefit from or even initiate dialogue; this distinguishes it from other uses of technology in education.
- The quasi-permanent absence of the learning group throughout the length of the learning process so that people are usually taught as individuals and not in groups, with the possibility of occasional meetings for both didactic and socialisation purposes.

(ibid., p. 49)

Keegan also adds two 'socio-cultural determinants' that he regards as 'both necessary pre-conditions and necessary consequences of distance education'. These are:

- the presence of more industrialised features than in conventional oral education;
- the privatisation of institutional learning. (ibid., p. 50)

Keegan's definition is more comprehensive than Holmberg's and it has been the subject of widespread discussion, criticism and amendment (Keegan 1989). Some have criticized Keegan's adoption of Peters' ideas regarding distance education as an industrialized form of education (Garrison and Shale 1990, Keegan 1994, Peters 1983); and/or the more modern version which portrays distance education as a Fordist form of production (Raggatt 1993, Rumble 1995). Some have seen distance education as involving a more general reconstruction of the time–space relations linking educational institutions and learners (Evans and Nation 1992). Others have sought instead to identify within distance education key dimensions such as communication, dialogue, structure, autonomy, independence and control (Moore 1990).

It may, however, be more realistic and pragmatic to regard distance education as simply 'education at a distance' (Garrison 1989: just as adult education may be interpreted as 'education for adults' – see Chapter 3). That is, distance education may be viewed as just one form of education, sharing the same key characteristics as all other forms:

All of what constitutes the process of education when teacher and student are able to meet face-to-face also constitutes the process of education when teacher and student are physically separated. All the necessary conditions for the educational process are inherent in face-to-face contact. They are not necessarily actualised, but the potential is always there. This is not the case when teacher and student are physically apart. The task of distance education is to find means by which to introduce these necessary conditions, or to simulate them so closely as to be acceptable proxies.

(Shale 1990, p. 334)

Perhaps the most telling criticism of the great majority of the definitions of distance education that have been offered is their idealization and unreality. There are few, if any, examples of institutions or courses which would meet in full the definitions of either Holmberg or Keegan. Thus, it does not seem necessary to require, as Keegan's first characteristic specifies, that teacher/ learner separation throughout the length of the learning process is the norm in distance education. Some elements or stages in the educational process may be carried out at a distance, some face-to-face, others by a mixture of these means. Indeed, in some institutions, both distance and face-to-face forms of provision may be offered, with a great deal of interchange and convergence in practice (Smith and Kelly 1987).

Similarly, the second of Keegan's characteristics seems to overplay, as does Holmberg's definition, the role and influence of educational organizations. This might in many cases be confined to particular, but perhaps critical, stages. Elements of private or independent study may also be incorporated within or alongside distance study. In the case of the third and fourth characteristics identified by Keegan, further reservations are also called for. After all, the technical media and two-way communication employed in distance education may in practice be minimal, and possibly absent entirely.

The more flexible conception that these criticisms imply suggests that in reality there is a continuous spectrum between face-to-face and distance forms of education (cf. the discussion of the education/learning and education/training spectra in Chapter 1). The ends of this spectrum are never encountered in practice, while along it there are no absolute dividing lines.

Many providers of distance education include elements, sometimes optional, sometimes compulsory, of face-to-face tuition within their programmes (e.g. Open University tutorials and summer schools). These may play a crucial role in the educational process. Perhaps more significantly, providers of distance education – in common with providers of face-to-face education

– typically expect their students to engage in varying amounts of private or independent study on their own and away from the direct influence of the teacher or the course text.

Distance education, practically defined, might then be seen as a form of education in which distance teaching techniques predominate, but not to the exclusion of other methods (Shale and Garrison 1990, Verduin and Clark 1991). Or, to put it in more contemporary terms, distance learning is 'The bringing together of teachers, learners, information, resources and learning support systems in a place (real or virtual) beyond the confines of the host institution' (Johnston 1997, pp. 107–8).

Open

> distance education and open learning are not interchangeable terms, for distance education does not necessarily embrace openness in terms of pace, access or learner-centredness.
> (Calder and McCollum 1998, p. 13)

The practice of 'openness' – the adoption of measures to encourage widespread access to and participation in education, training and learning – by universities, schools and other educational institutions is, contrary to received wisdom, of long standing (Bell and Tight 1993, Nyberg 1975). Yet, the encapsulation of these practices in a general philosophy of 'open learning' appears to be a relatively recent development (Bosworth 1991, Tait 1993, Thorpe and Grugeon 1987). Open learning is also, like distance education, the subject of fierce debate (see, for example, Boot and Hodgson 1987, Rumble 1989).

Of the many definitions of 'open learning' which have been put forward during the last two decades, the following are not untypical:

> 'Open learning' is a term used to describe courses flexibly designed to meet individual requirements. It is often applied to provision which tries to remove barriers that prevent attendances at more traditional courses, but it also suggests a learner-centred philosophy. Open-learning courses may be offered in a learning centre of some kind or most of the activity may be carried out away from such a centre (e.g. at home). In nearly every case specially prepared or adapted materials are necessary.
> (Lewis and Spencer 1986, pp. 9–10)

Open learning is merely one of the most recent manifestations of a gradual trend towards the democratisation of education. The use of the term 'open' admits that education and learning have traditionally been 'closed' by various barriers – entrance requirements, time constraints, financial demands, geographical distances, and, much more subtly, social and cultural barriers, as well as those of gender. An open learning institution is one dedicated to helping individuals overcome these barriers to their further education.

(Paul 1990, p. 42)

Both of the authors quoted fall into the trap of seeing the practice, as distinct from the nomenclature, of open learning as a recent development, to be contrasted favourably with a 'traditional' and 'closed' approach (see the discussion of tensions, traditions and dichotomies in Chapter 3). Lewis's definition may also be faulted for putting too much emphasis on specially prepared materials, which need not be seen as essential, and thereby linking open learning too closely to distance education.

Both definitions characterize open learning as being about the removal of barriers. These barriers can be classified broadly into three groups:

- physical/temporal: those restricting the time, place and pace at which learning may be undertaken;
- individual/social: those to do with the characteristics of individual learners (e.g. age, sex, ethnicity, class, wealth);
- learning: those to do with the nature of the learning provided (e.g. content, structure, delivery, accreditation, flexibility).

Open educational or training institutions are in the business not just of removing some or all of these barriers, but of going further to adopt positive, outgoing and involving attitudes, practices and images to the community at large (see also the discussion of social inclusion in Chapter 7).

It would be foolish, of course, to imagine that any one educational institution or provider could realistically attempt to be wholly open in all of these ways. Most of those who see themselves as being involved in open learning have focused their openness on a particular group or set of characteristics, and remain relatively 'closed' in other ways (Harris 1987).

This has not prevented the launch of a proliferation of programmes and institutions with the word 'open' in their titles since the 1980s, many of them short-lived. Thus, in the United Kingdom, the national Open College (Corlett 1998), various regional Open Colleges or Open College Federations and Networks, the Open Learning Foundation, the Open Polytechnic and the Open Tech have all followed the lead of the Open University. The naming of the British Open University itself led to an understandable confusion between the two terms 'distance education' and 'open learning', which some have taken as virtually synonymous. But the messages conveyed through the word 'open' are clearly just too good to miss:

> Open learning is an imprecise phrase to which a range of meanings can be, and is, attached. It eludes definition. But as an inscription to be carried in procession on a banner, gathering adherents and enthusiasms, it has great potential. For its very imprecision enables it to accommodate many different ideas and aims.
>
> (Mackenzie, Postgate and Scupham 1975, p. 15)

Most worrying, perhaps, is the use of open learning to refer to the use of learning packages designed to impart work-related skills cheaply and with minimal support (McNay 1988). In the 1980s, open learning, in this narrow sense, was increasingly adopted in the United Kingdom by both industry and government as a cost-effective substitute for more conventional forms of training: 'ideas originating in the quite different context of opening up access for adults to higher education have been imported into training for teenagers in work-related skills (Bynner 1992, p. 105).

In practice – as in the case of distance, face-to-face and private education – we should probably view all educational providers as operating somewhere along a spectrum between 'open-ness' and 'closure' (Lewis 1986).

Flexible

The use of the term 'flexible learning' has been closely associated in the United Kingdom with the further education sector. Its development was particularly linked to the work of the former Further Education Unit (FEU). The concept has been simply defined by the FEU as 'the adaptation of available learning opportunities to meet the needs of the learner in a way that optimises the autonomy of the learner as well as the effectiveness of the process of learning' (FEU 1983, p. 11).

The FEU also identified a series of dimensions of practice along which the degree of flexibility practised by an educational or training provider may be judged. These include the aims and content of learning, the characteristics and stage of development of the learner on entry, the mode of learning, the resources available for training, mode of attendance, pace of learning, interactions with others and methods of assessment (FEU 1984).

The idea of flexible learning, like open learning, has received the backing of the British government and been incorporated in various government funded initiatives designed to develop skills in the labour force (Department of Employment 1991). It has been linked to analogous ideas about flexible labour and organizations (Edwards 1997, Felstead and Jewson 1999, Pollert 1991). Most recently, it has been increasingly applied in higher education (Thomas 1995, Wade *et al.* 1994).

Like open learning and distance education, the concept of flexible learning has been the subject of both misuse and critique. Thus, each of these three terms has been associated by some specifically with the development of learning materials, an association not unconnected with the desire of educational organizations and their funders to be more cost effective. Its advocates, however, see flexible learning in a different light:

> flexible learning is essentially student-centred learning, and is about meeting student needs using whatever methods of teaching and learning are most appropriate ... [it is not] concerned mainly with the use of specially prepared resource-based learning materials designed to replace tutor contact.
>
> (Hudson, Maslin-Prothero and Oates 1997, p. 3)

> Flexible learning is a movement away from a situation in which key decisions about learning dimensions are made in advance by the instructor or institution, towards a situation where the learner has a range of options from which to choose with respect to these key dimensions.
>
> (Collis and Moonen 2001, p. 10)

Indeed, the idea of student-centred learning, or even learner-centred learning, is probably now in the process of supplanting flexible learning as the more acceptable term.

Critique has focused most tellingly on the notion, whether implied or explicit, that flexible learning is radically new and better than existing alternatives:

the tendency seems to be to present flexible learning unproblematically as a new technology for the delivery of learning which increases overall access to the system and choice for the individual within it. It is therefore dominantly positioned as a 'better' form of delivery for learning rather than anything that may possibly change the content or outcomes of learning itself, or have significant effects on society.

(Nicoll 1997, p. 100)

EXPERIENTIAL, PROBLEM-BASED, INDEPENDENT AND SELF-DIRECTED

The second group of learning concepts to be considered in this chapter differs from the first in focusing more on the perspective of the individual learner than on that of the organization providing the learning opportunities. As already suggested, however, this distinction is by no means clear-cut.

Four concepts will be considered in some detail in this section in two linked pairs: experiential and problem-based learning, and independent and self-directed learning. As with the organizational group, there are a number of other related concepts in common use. These include action and discovery learning, which are most closely related to the concepts of experiential and problem-based learning; and autonomous, individualized and learner-managed learning, which have close affinities with the ideas of independent and self-directed learning (e.g. Graves 1993, Long 1990, Tait and Knight 1996).

Resource-based and student-centred learning (Brandes and Ginnis 1986, Brown and Smith 1996), mentioned in the previous section, are also related to the latter pairing, demonstrating that many of these concepts can be approached from either an individual or an organizational perspective.

Experiential and problem-based

A number of different uses of the concept of experiential learning are current. One recent study identified four main interpretations, emphasizing the role of experiential learning as:

- the assessment and accreditation of learning from life and work experience;
- a means of bringing about changes in the structures, purposes and curricula of post-school education;
- a basis for group consciousness raising, community action and social change; or
- a means for increasing self awareness and group effectiveness.

(Weil and McGill 1989).

These interpretations were then associated with the work of particular authors, including, respectively, Evans, Kolb, Freire (see the later discussion of conscientization in this chapter) and Rogers.

Kolb's work on the theoretical foundations of experiential learning can be seen to underlie most, if not all, approaches in this area. It has also been influential in developing our broader understanding of the nature of learning (see the section on learning in Chapter 1). Kolb builds on Lewin's four-stage feedback model of learning, which involves concrete experience, observation and reflection, the formation of abstract concepts and generalizations, and the testing of the implications of these in new situations (Kolb 1984). This simple model of learning has been very influential amongst adult educators and trainers (e.g. Boud, Cohen and Walker 1993, Boud and Miller 1996, Burnard 1988). It is not, however, without its critics:

> the concept of experiential learning, in the form used by Kolb and the adult education tradition, represents the kind of psychological reductionism that Dewey considered a misrepresentation of his antidualist conception of experience. This conception is based in Kolb's book on the model of a very particular historical incident – or habit: the immediate feedback in human relation training. Although this procedure has developed into one of the tenets of T-group training, it is epistemologically highly problematic and cannot be generalized as a way in which people learn.
>
> (Miettinen 2000, p. 70)

Whether over-simplistic and over-particular or not, the influence of Kolb's model can be seen, for example, in the movement to enable the accreditation or assessment of prior learning, or of prior experiential learning (abbreviated as APL, APEL and various similar acronyms: see also the discussion of accreditation in Chapter 7). This movement has achieved particular prominence during the last two decades, having been imported into the United Kingdom and other countries from the United States of America. It starts from the recognition or assumption that many adults possess considerable knowledge, understanding or skills, often developed through work, social or voluntary activities, which has not been, but is worthy of, accreditation towards an appropriate qualification (Evans 1992, 2000).

Evans has defined the concept as follows:

> Experiential Learning means the knowledge and skills acquired through life and work experience and study which are not formally attested through any educational or professional certification ... Hence the assessment of prior experiential learning (APEL) refers to all learning which has not been assessed. This marks it off from the assessment of prior learning (APL), which also includes learning which has been assessed for some formal purpose.
>
> (Evans 1994, p. 1)

The various methods involved in producing and assessing evidence of prior learning are now widely understood and accepted. However, their implementation remains patchy. While APL and APEL have made inroads into further education, where they are seen as one more means of developing flexibility, they have yet to be so widely accepted in higher education (Challis 1993, Field 1993, Simosko 1991).

The third and fourth interpretations of experiential learning identified by Weil and McGill are particularly associated with more 'traditional' or radical forms of adult education (see the discussion of adult and continuing in Chapter 3). The former interpretation would typically seek to embody a recognition of the value of each individual adult's experience, and then endeavour to use and build upon it in the learning experience. The latter would include, for example, initiatives with women's, black or working-class groups.

But other uses of the term are also current. For example, experiential learning has been defined as 'synonymous with 'meaningful-discovery' learning ... This is learning which involves the learner in sorting things out for himself [sic], by restructuring his perceptions of what is happening' (Boydell

1976, p. 19). In this form the concept has been linked with autonomous, integrative and action learning (McGill and Beaty 1992, Revans 1982). It has become influential within management development thinking (Kolb *et al.* 1986), and has contributed to the articulation of the idea of the learning organization (see Chapter 2).

Problem-based learning can be seen as an educational approach that makes deliberate use of the learning strategies suggested by theories of experiential learning. In other words, by using realistic problems – of the kind the learner is likely to encounter in their current or future workplace – as the basis for learning, practical experience and a deeper understanding of the relation between practice and theory can be developed in the individual. Problem-based learning has strong roots in medical education, with some departments and faculties organizing all of their instruction on this basis, but has also been applied to other forms of education and training, particularly those concerned with developing professionals.

The key features of problem-based learning as an educational approach have been summarized as follows:

- using stimulus material to help students discuss an important problem, question or issue;
- presenting the problem as a simulation of professional practice or a 'real life' situation;
- appropriately guiding students' critical thinking and providing limited resources to help them learn from defining and attempting to resolve the given problem;
- having students work cooperatively as a group, exploring information in and out of class, with access to a tutor (not necessarily a subject specialist) who knows the problem well and can facilitate the group's learning process;
- getting students to identify their own learning needs and appropriate use of available resources;
- reapplying this new knowledge to the original problem and evaluating their learning processes.

(Boud and Feletti 1998, p. 2)

Many of these features – e.g. collaborative group work, identifying individual needs, relating learning to life – would, of course, be seen as good practice in most forms and levels of education and training. The distinctive feature of problem-based

learning is the focusing of the learning process on the identification, exploration and attempted resolution of realistic problems.
Learning is then explicitly structured as the kind of circular or
spiral process envisaged in Kolb's model.
Problem-based learning has been promoted by another of its
proponents on the grounds that it:

- encourages open-minded, reflective, critical and active
  learning . . .
- is morally defensible in that it pays due respect to both
  student and teacher as persons with knowledge, understanding, feelings and interests who come together in a
  shared educational process . . .
- reflects the nature of knowledge – that is, knowledge
  is complex and changes as a result of responses by
  communities or persons to problems they perceive in their
  worlds.

(Margetson 1997, p. 39)

All of these may be good points, of course, but they are hardly
confined to problem-based learning.

Independent and self-directed

The history of adult educational discourse surrounding
self-directed learning demonstrates, depending on one's
viewpoint, either its remarkable conceptual utility, or the
co-optation and enslavement by corporate capitalism of a once
subversive idea. From being regarded as a vaguely anarchistic,
Illich-inspired threat to formal adult education, self-direction
is now comfortably ensconced in the citadel, firmly part of
the conceptual and practical mainstream.

(Brookfield 2000, p. 9)

The concepts of independent and self-directed learning are so
closely linked that they will be treated here as essentially synonymous. They have obvious connections with the practice of
distance education, discussed earlier in this chapter. In distance
education, the learner and teacher are normally separated in both
space and time, so that the distant learner is also to a greater
extent independent or self-directed. However, like open learning,
these concepts have a broader association as well. That is, they
refer to all cases where the responsibility for, and control of, the

learning experience – its planning, delivery and assessment – is largely transferred from the institution to the individual learner.

Historically, the idea of self-directed learning is particularly associated with the work of Tough, who carried out and inspired a body of empirical research in the 1970s and 1980s (Tough 1971, 1989). Tough believed that much significant learning was carried out by individual adults in the form of learning projects, largely outside of the influence of formal educational institutions (cf. informal learning, discussed in Chapter 3). He defined a learning project as a 'highly deliberate effort to gain and retain certain knowledge or skill', and set an arbitrary minimum length of seven hours. From his studies, Tough estimated that the average adult conducted eight learning projects lasting 700 hours in total in a year. Of these, two-thirds were planned by the learner, and only one-fifth by a professional educator. The most common motivation for learning was some anticipated use or application of knowledge or skill, with less than 1 per cent of projects being undertaken for credit.

The research of Tough and his followers has been influential, but has also been criticized:

> self-directed learning has been critiqued in many ways. Theoretically it assumes a unitary self able to make rational and coherent choices . . . Moreover, self-directed learning has not given rise to practices which are necessarily emancipatory . . . in its emphasis on the individual, it marginalises the significance of the collective and the co-operative. In its emphasis on emancipatory choice it leads to students demanding whatever it is that they feel is their 'right' in terms of educational fodder. In its emphasis on the responsible, self-motivated adult, it is used by governments to argue that adult education does not need resourcing.
>
> (Hughes 1999, p. 7)

Other criticisms have included the focus of most of the research on middle-class respondents, the tendency to reduce their experiences to quantitative measures rather than exploring the quality of the learning engaged in, and the lack of attention given to the implications of the research findings (Brookfield 1984, Taylor 2000).

Both Hughes, in her final point, and Brookfield, in the quotation which opens this section, suggest that self-direction is a politically charged concept. Brookfield takes this further:

The case for self-direction as an inherently political concept rests on two arguments. First, that at the heart of self-direction are issues of power and control, particularly regarding the definition of acceptable and appropriate learning activities. Who defines the boundaries of intellectual inquiry is always a political question, and self-direction places this decision squarely in the hands of learners. Second, exercising self-direction inevitably requires certain conditions to be in place regarding access to resources, conditions that are essentially political in nature. Claiming the resources needed to conduct self-directed learning can be regarded as a political act.

(Brookfield 2000, p. 16)

In the contemporary world, therefore, self-directed learning chimes in well with the overall socio-economic policies of neo-liberal, New Right and New Labour governments (see also the discussion of lifelong learning and the learning society in Chapter 2). But, in practice, the promotion of self-directed learning may be more about transferring the costs of learning to learners, rather than making additional resources available for support:

If, until the nineties, the idea of self-directed learning necessarily went hand in hand with that of intentional learning, such is no longer the case. In the context of heavy pressure on learning and skill development, combined with growing needs to be satisfied, and stagnant, if not dwindling training budgets, one can perceive hints of the paradoxical notion of 'compulsory self-directed learning'.

(Carré 2000, pp. 50–1)

Yet, even if adults accepted the need to engage in self-directed learning, and to at least partially resource such efforts themselves, it may be questioned whether they will all be able to meet the demands this imposes upon them as individuals. Thus, for adult educators, while self-directed learning implies a move from teacher to facilitator, this need not mean that their teaching or training role will disappear (Boud and Higgs 1993, Titmus 1999).

ANDRAGOGY, CONSCIENTIZATION AND COMMUNITIES OF PRACTICE

The first two concepts discussed in this section share a number of characteristics. They both came to prominence in the

English-speaking world in the 1960s and 1970s. They both derived from non-Western sources: andragogy stemming from Eastern Europe and conscientization from Brazil. They both made their chief proponents – Malcolm Knowles in the case of andragogy and Paulo Freire in the case of conscientization – famous, at least within the world of adult education and training.

However, while it would be difficult to ignore these concepts in a book of this nature, they may both now be seen as somewhat dated and out of fashion. When they were first articulated in the West, they had a radical feel to them. This has now either become compromised or has been over-ridden by more pragmatic interests. Hence the inclusion of a third concept in this section – communities of practice – one that has a much more contemporary feel to it, and which promises much for future theoretical developments.

Andragogy

> Malcolm Knowles's formulation of andragogy was the first major attempt in the West to construct a comprehensive theory of adult education ... While it was not as comprehensive a theory as he would have perhaps anticipated, he provided a baseline for considerable discussion about the nature of adult education.
>
> (Jarvis 2001a, p. 157)

The concept of andragogy – whether seen as a theory, a set of hypotheses or just as guidelines for practice – has been the subject of extensive discussion over the last three decades: 'this concept is the single most popular idea in the education and training of adults, in part because and for the way in which it grants to educators of adults a sense of their distinct professional identity' (Brookfield 1986, p. 91).

Though the term originates from Europe (Krajnc 1989), it owes its later development and popularity to the work of an American adult educator, Malcolm Knowles (Knowles 1970, 1973, 1985). He defined andragogy, in contra-distinction to pedagogy, rather loosely as 'the art and science of helping adults learn'. While Knowles' interpretation and application of the concept have varied somewhat over the years, a series of assumptions about individual adult learning have remained at the core:

as a person matures:

1 his [sic] self-concept moves from one of being a dependent personality toward one of being a self-directed human being;

2 he accumulates a growing reservoir of experience that becomes an increasing resource for learning;

3 his readiness to learn becomes oriented increasingly to the developmental tasks of his social roles; and

4 his time perspective changes from one of postponed application of knowledge to immediacy of application, and accordingly his orientation toward learning shifts from one of subject-centredness to one of problem-centredness.
(Knowles 1970, quoted in Tight 1983, p. 55)

The links to more recent notions about experiential and self-directed learning, discussed in the previous section, are clear. Knowles then went on to identify 'conditions of learning' for adults, together with associated 'principles of teaching', thereby providing explicit guidance as to how the theory should be applied in practice.

While Knowles' arguments for andragogy have met with considerable enthusiasm and support on both sides of the Atlantic (e.g. Allman 1983, Mezirow 1981), they have also, of course, been the subject of much criticism (e.g. Brookfield 1986, Tennant 1997). These critiques have tackled the underlying assumptions of andragogy one by one. Thus, the widespread existence of self-direction amongst adults (see the previous section), and its implied absence in children, has been queried. Similarly, the problem-centred focus (also discussed in the previous section) of adult, as opposed to child, learning has been questioned. The third assumption has been seen as ignoring the reflective, personal and serendipitous aspects of adult learning, while suggesting a reductionist and behaviouristic, competency-based approach to practice (see the discussion of competence in Chapter 6).

Of the four assumptions, it is the second that has been least criticized: 'it is this second assumption of andragogy that can arguably lay claim to be viewed as being a "given" in the literature of adult learning' (Brookfield 1986, p. 98). Yet, even in this case, the significance of the assumption for adult education and training practice has been doubted: 'experience may well be a characteristic that sets children apart from adults, but it is not a characteristic which is relevant in distinguishing between good educational practice for adults and good educational practice for children' (Tennant 1998, p. 21).

But the importance of this assumption, even if only as an assertive device of difference, remains strong amongst practitioners:

> in the andragogical tradition, experience is at the centre of knowledge production and acquisition. Using experience becomes not simply a pedagogical device but more significantly an affirmation of the ontological and ethical status of adults, in particular, the mark of their radical difference from children.
>
> (Usher, Bryant and Johnston 1997, p. 95)

After such a barrage of criticism, there may seem to be little left for the concept of andragogy:

> Given the semantical problems in Knowles's definition of andragogy, the lack of clarity and specificity in his underlying assumptions, the research reports which do not support and sometimes even refute it, and the mounting academic criticism of it as a legitimate theory or approach, one might ask if andragogy retains any utility or viability for the discipline of adult education.
>
> (Davenport 1987, p. 19)

Yet that author still saw a role for andragogy, suitably refined and redefined, recognizing the public relations value of the concept. There seems to have been less discussion of andragogy in adult education and training circles over the last few years. It can reasonably be concluded that any aspirations for presenting andragogy as an over-arching theory are now gone, though it retains some value as a guide to practice, and remains popular in some areas.

Conscientization

The term conscientization is closely associated with the work of Paulo Freire, a Brazilian adult educator who has achieved worldwide renown. The work through which Freire developed his conceptual ideas was carried out in the poorer areas of Recifé, in north-east Brazil, and had a particular focus on developing the literacy of men. It extended far beyond the inculcation of basic skills, however, to concern itself with broader themes of individual emancipation and community empowerment. Given these concerns, it is not surprising that Freire ran into political opposition, and spent many years in exile in other countries. Freire's work and writing is probably the best example in the field of adult education and training of ideas from the developing world coming to have a major influence in the industrialized world. It raises the issue of whether such cultural transfers are either practical or useful, as Freire's methods have been adopted and adapted with mixed success in many countries (e.g. Kirkwood and Kirkwood 1989, Mackie 1980, Mayo 1999, McLaren and Lankshear 1994). More specifically, since Freire wrote in Portuguese, and has been read by most people in translation, it may be that something has been lost in that process.

Thus, Freire himself always used the Portuguese term *conscientização* rather than the most obvious or convenient English translation, 'conscientization', which is repeated here. His two most influential books, both now about thirty years old, define this term in the following, somewhat divergent but complementary, ways:

> *Conscientização* is the deepening of the attitude of awareness characteristic of all emergence ... In contrast with the anti-dialogical and non-communicative 'deposits' of the banking method of education, the programme content of the problem-posing method – dialogical par excellence – is constituted and organised by the student's view of the world, where their own generative themes are found.
>
> (Freire 1972, p. 101)

> *Conscientização* represents the *development* of the awakening of critical awareness. It will not appear as a natural byproduct of even major economic changes, but must grow out of a critical educational effort based on favourable historical conditions.
>
> (Freire 1974, p. 19, original emphasis)

The concept is articulated in opposition to what Freire calls the 'banking' method of education; in other words, the notion that students' minds are 'empty vessels' to be filled up by the wisdom and expertise of their teachers. For Freire, true education or learning is about dialogue, and is about giving students space and support to develop their ideas and themselves within, and against the background of, their social, political and economic context.

For others, the real power of this idea lies not just in the process itself, but in the transformation it may bring about in the learner. 'Conscientization is a process of developing consciousness, but consciousness that is understood to have the power to transform reality' (Taylor 1993, p. 52).

Clearly, there are many linkages between Freire's idea of *conscientização* and other contemporary educational concepts. Freire himself makes the link with critical consciousness, and others have made a connection with consciousness raising, with its particular associations in the 1970s in the West with the women's movement (Mezirow 1981). The related notion of education as being about individual and collective emancipation or empowerment have also already been mentioned, though linking conscientization with enlightenment may be going too far (Matthews 1980).

The linkages are, however, much broader than this:

> The idea of analysing one's experiences to achieve liberation from psychological repression or social and political oppression is a recurring theme in adult education. It is most commonly associated with the work of Freire but it is also a feature of some contemporary conceptions of self-directed learning, andragogy, action research, models of the learning process and techniques of facilitation.
>
> (Tennant 1997, p. 123)

This effectively associates Freire with some of the most widely regarded western adult educators, including Knowles and Tough. It also makes Freire's position apparent in the debate about the respective roles of teacher and learner (see the sections on learning and teaching in Chapter 1).

Like Freire, both Knowles and Tough came to prominence a few decades ago. Though their place in the adult education Hall of Fame seems assured, their ideas about the curriculum have been supplanted in the political consciousness by other concepts. These concepts – such as capability, enterprise, competence and quality (all discussed in Chapter 6) – have a harder and more pragmatic ring to them (but see Carmen 1995, Gibson 1994). Set against them, conscientization seems in some ways to be even more radical than it was in the 1960s.

Communities of practice

The notion of communities of practice has come to prominence in the last decade or so (Lave and Wenger 1991). It can be seen as a kind of middle way for studying adult learning, focusing neither on the individual or the organization, but on the group. While linked to ideas like experiential learning, self-directed learning and conscientization (discussed earlier in this chapter), communities of practice offer a new project for both understanding how learning takes place in its context and supporting that learning.

Communities of practice have been defined in the following way:

> Communities-of-practice are the relationships people strike up to solve problems (though they may be influenced by formal role relationships as well). Within communities-of-practice, people share tacit knowledge and through dialogue bring this to the surface; they exchange ideas about work practice and experiment with new methods and ideas; they innovate new problem-solving techniques and simultaneously manage and repair the social context. In other words, they engage in experiential learning, develop and refine cognitive structures, and engage in culture formation. Through linked communities-of-practice, knowledge, rules for action, and culture are spread.
> (Hendry 1996, p. 628)

Communities of practice appear, therefore, to be more than just another learning concept. There are further links here to ideas such as informal learning (see Chapter 3), and to ideas about the development and use of human and social capital (see Chapter 4). Yet, while the primary application of the concept to date has been to understanding learning in the workplace, particularly in a professional context (see Chapter 4), there is no reason why it cannot be applied to learning in social contexts more broadly as well:

> Communities of practice are the basic building blocks of a social learning system because they are the social 'containers'

of the competences that make up such a system. By participating in these communities, we define with each other what
constitutes competence in a given context: being a reliable
doctor, a gifted photographer, a popular student, or an astute
poker player ... Communities of practice define competence
by combining three elements. First, members are bound
together by their collectively developed understanding of
what their community is about and they hold each other
accountable to this sense of *joint enterprise*. To be competent
is to understand the enterprise well enough to be able to
contribute to it. Second, members build their community
through mutual engagement. They interact with one another,
establishing norms and relationships of *mutuality* that reflect
these interactions. To be competent is to be able to engage
with the community and be trusted as a partner in these
interactions. Third, communities of practice have produced a
shared repertoire of communal resources – language, routines,
sensibilities, artefacts, tools, stories, styles, etc. To be competent is to have access to this repertoire and be able to use it
appropriately.

(Wenger 2000, p. 229, original emphasis)

Though the use of the term competence (see Chapter 6) may
again suggest a vocational context, the articulation of the three
component elements of communities of practice as joint enterprise, mutuality and shared repertoire argues for a broader
application. Seen from this perspective, the development of a
learning society (see Chapter 2) could be seen as being largely
about the development and support of a multitude of communities of practice throughout work and society.

CHANGING INFORMATION AND COMMUNICATION TECHNOLOGIES

All of the concepts discussed in this chapter are clearly more or
less closely related to each other. Whether their major focus is
on the institutional provider of learning opportunities, or on the
individual learner, they all present idealizations of how adult
learning and training might best be delivered. It might reasonably be questioned, therefore, why there appear to be so many
competing concepts in this area.

Historically, at least three possible, and partial, explanations suggest themselves. First, we are here dealing with groups of concepts that have been advanced over a period of decades, and that have come to prominence in different countries. Second, we have to recognize the breadth and looseness of the field of adult education and training, between some areas of which there may be relatively little communication. Third, to these reasons we need to add an appreciation of the politics of the field being studied. Put simply, the organizations and individuals that develop and promote particular learning concepts will have put a lot of work and commitment into them, and are unlikely to be willing to see them subsumed into more generally accepted terms without considerable resistance.

In the contemporary climate, a fourth, related reason for the proliferation of learning concepts may also be recognized. This has to do with the ideology of change, and its practical manifestation in the realm of technology. Earlier in this chapter, it was noted that the concepts of correspondence, distance and open education or learning were linked together in a developmental sense, and that there were some who suggested that a fourth generation of learning technology was manifesting itself in computer-based learning.

This kind of thinking often underlies the breathless prose of technophiles, whose enthusiasm for the latest development in information and communication technologies can lead them to believe that some kind of quick technical 'fix' is possible to resolve society's learning problems:

> The past 30 years have witnessed an amazing revolution in teaching and training around the world. Whilst forms of correspondence teaching have been practised for thousands of years, and refined during the last century in various correspondence courses, it was the creation of the Open University in 1969 that signalled a major change in the way teaching and learning was organized and practised. Since the creation of the Open University, Open, Distance, Flexible, Resource Based – and now Distributed Learning – have expanded dramatically around the world ... At the present time we are poised on the threshold of another revolution, one involving Communication and Information Technology and the Knowledge Media, which will have a profound effect on teaching and learning for all of us.
>
> (Lockwood 2001, p. 1)

While recognizing that new technologies offer new opportunities, one does not have to be a technophobe to see problems with the kind of prospectus being outlined here. On the one hand, we may note that in many cases more basic learning technologies may be just as or more appropriate, and that both learners and teachers may reject more advanced aids:

In the recent past, several new technologies – film, radio, television and, more recently, computers and CD-ROMs – have been hailed as agents of educational transformation. And yet education – or at least formal education as practised in schools and colleges – has remained stubbornly resistant to radical change. Notwithstanding the adoption of some significant, if peripheral, aids – the overhead projector, xerographic reproduction of lecture notes, and the pocket calculator – the process of teaching in universities and colleges has continued largely unchanged for the last century or more.

(Curran 2001, p. 113)

On the other hand, bearing in mind the existing distribution of resources and opportunities throughout society (see the discussion of access and participation, and of social inclusion, in Chapter 7), we may doubt the applicability of technological solutions to all learning problems: 'an archetypal example of the "technical fix" underlies the notion that technology will overcome barriers to learning in "helping" individual learners over-come pre-existing problems' (Selwyn, Goran and Williams 2001, p. 260). Many more learning concepts will, doubtless, be developed and promoted in the years to come, but we will need to continue to keep a sense of perspective regarding their practical value.

FURTHER READING

Boud, D, and Feletti (eds) (1997) *The Challenge of Problem-based Learning*. London, Kogan Page, second edition.
   Good collection of articles on theory and practice.
Garrison, D (1989) *Understanding Distance Education: a framework for the future*. London, Routledge.
   One of the most accessible accounts of this field, which is sensibly modest in the claims that it makes.
Jarvis, P (ed.) (2001) *Twentieth Century Thinkers in Adult and Continuing Education*. London, Kogan Page, second edition.

Contains a measured assessment of the work, influence and position of Freire and Knowles, amongst others.

Straka, G (ed.) (2000) *Conceptions of Self-directed Learning: theoretical and conceptual considerations.* Munster, Waxmann.

Useful review of contemporary thinking on this concept.

Tait, A (ed.) (1993) *Key Issues in Open Learning: a reader. An anthology from the journal 'Open Learning', 1986–1992.* Harlow, Longman.

A selection of articles from the journal based at the British Open University: not surprisingly, a lot of the papers chosen focus on distance education, and on the Open University in particular.

Weil, S and McGill, I (eds) (1989) *Making Sense of Experiential Learning: diversity in theory and practice.* Milton Keynes, Open University Press.

A thoughtful study of different interpretations of the term, arguing for the need to understand and share different perspectives.

Chapter 6

Curricular Concepts

DEVELOPING THE CURRICULUM

> we will understand by the term 'curriculum' the overall ratio-
> nale for any educational programme, including those more
> subtle features of curriculum change and development and
> especially those underlying principles which ... are the most
> crucial element in curriculum studies.
>
> (Kelly 1999, p. 3)

Curriculum development, which is concerned with the aims,
processes and outcomes of educational provision, has become
an area of increasing importance within adult education and
training over the last few decades (Squires 1987, 1990). Two main,
linked reasons for this may be identified: the overall rise in levels
of provision and participation, and the increased interest taken
by the government and other external authorities in the nature
of the education and training being delivered. What is taught,
and how it is taught, are currently seen as being issues of more
general concern, and not to be left to individual teachers or
lecturers, their employers or institutions.

As in the case of many of the other areas considered in this book,
there is an extensive range of concepts in use, of which only some
will be analysed here. The term curriculum is itself, of course, a
concept of note. It is one which has been extensively discussed
from a school-based perspective, though less so by adult educators (Griffin 1983). There are a number of tensions evident within
these discussions between differing views of the curriculum:

- curriculum as an area of study (i.e. a syllabus) or all of an
  educational institution's activities;

- curriculum as content, product or process; and
- the formal, informal and hidden elements of the curriculum.

(Kelly 1999)

The approach taken in this chapter will be both broad, in its interpretation of the scope of the curriculum, and selective, in its choice of concepts for examination. The emphasis will be on overall approaches to the curriculum, rather than particular aspects of its planning, delivery or evaluation. The chapter starts with what may be seen as the more 'traditional' concepts of knowledge and skill. These concepts can be seen to underpin all adult education and training, as well as embodying some of the opposition (see the section 'vocational or liberal?' in Chapter 1) evident between education and training.

The remainder of the chapter will then focus on four concepts that have a rather different feel to them. Though by no means new, they have come into, or back into, prominence during the last two decades. These concepts are those of competence, capability, enterprise and quality. They share the characteristic of resulting largely from the intervention within education and training of outside interests.

KNOWLEDGE AND SKILL

Type A knowledge is defined in terms of propositional knowledge, codified and stored in publications, libraries, databases, etc., subject to quality control by editors and peer review, and given foundational status by incorporation into examinations and qualifications. Under this definition, skills are regarded as separate from knowledge ... Type B knowledge is defined in terms of personal knowledge – i.e. what people bring to practical situations that enables them to think and perform. Such personal knowledge is acquired not only through the use of public knowledge but is also constructed from personal experience and reflection. It includes propositional knowledge along with procedural and process knowledge, tacit knowledge, and experiential knowledge in episodic memory. Under this definition, skills are treated as part of knowledge rather than as separate from it.

(Eraut 1997, p. 552)

The concepts of knowledge and skill have a long history and a widespread common usage, and, as Eraut suggests, are inextricably linked together. As already suggested, they can also be seen as representative of the perceived dichotomy between education and training. They are not, of course, the only such oppositional terms. With a little thought, a list can readily be compiled (see Figure 6.1).

education	versus	**training**
knowledge	versus	**skill**
understanding	versus	**experience**
theory	versus	**practice**
academic	versus	**vocational**

Figure 6.1 Conceptual dichotomies

To take this presentation a little further, the latter (right hand) of each pair can be seen as useful, public, external and to do with the 'real' world, while the former may be caricatured as useless, elitist, internal and within the ivory tower. Such caricatures are only such, of course, and fall down as soon as any more detailed analysis is engaged in. Yet, they do have purchase and influence, and are not so far away from being the views of many of those with power to influence education and training.

What, then, is meant by knowledge? More absolutist and objective conceptions of knowledge are still, of course, adhered to by many, particularly those coming from a background in the pure sciences. Others, including the present author, lean towards more relativistic and changing perceptions. This is not to deny the power of science, however, or its general view of its subject matter as potentially entirely knowable, but to recognize that such an approach does not work from all disciplinary perspectives. Sociologists, for example, will typically see knowledge, like truth, as socially constructed (Blackledge and Hunt 1985). Many philosophers see it as inseparably connected with power:

> Knowledge, therefore, does not simply represent the truth of what is but, rather, constitutes what is taken to be true

... Thus, rather than taking changes in knowledge as the progressive unfolding of truth, it is necessary to examine the complex exercise of power which is immanent in such changes.

(Usher and Edwards 1994, pp. 87–8)

Much recent research and writing on knowledge seeks to distinguish between different types of knowledge. Thus, in the quote that opens this section, Eraut distinguishes between propositional knowledge – which might be characterized as academic and factual – and personal knowledge, that which is held and used by individuals. He further divides the latter to include not just elements of propositional knowledge, but also procedural, process, tacit and experiential knowledges (cf. the discussion of experiential learning in Chapter 5). In earlier research on managers, he identified six types of knowledge: situational, people, practice, conceptual, process and control; which, he claimed, might be generally applicable, at least to other professions (Eraut 1990, 1994).

An alternative perspective on, and categorization of, knowledge starts from the recognition that the 'traditional' producers and assessors of propositional knowledge, the universities, are under increasing challenge from other institutions and groups (e.g. private companies, community groups). This situation is seen as being particularly competitive at a time when the possession and development of useful knowledge is of increasing importance:

the parallel expansion in the number of potential knowledge producers on the supply side and the expansion of the requirement of specialist knowledge on the demand side are creating the conditions for the emergence of a new mode of knowledge production.

(Gibbons et al. 1994, p. 13)

As a consequence, it is argued, there are now two main kinds of knowledge:

By contrast with traditional knowledge, which we will call Mode 1, generated within a disciplinary, primarily cognitive, context, Mode 2 knowledge is created in broader, transdisciplinary social and economic contexts ... The emergence of Mode 2 ... is profound and calls into question the adequacy of familiar knowledge producing institutions, whether universities, government research establishments, or corporate laboratories ... in Mode 1 problems are set and solved in a context governed by the, largely academic, interests of a specific community. By contrast, Mode 2 knowledge is carried out in a context of application.

(ibid., pp. 1, 3)

These kinds of arguments are currently both popular and influential (see also Nowotny, Scott and Gibbons 2001). However, they do not seem to be saying more (indeed, it could be argued they are saying less, or are saying something rather different) than Eraut and others have been saying for some time, and in a more measured way.

The notion of skill also presents problems with different disciplinary definitions and interests:

Labour economists generally see skill as a property of an individual, made up of various combinations of education, training and competence. Industrial sociologists, on the other hand, have normally regarded skill as an aspect of jobs themselves, derived from the imperatives of industrial and technological organisation, without giving much attention to the relations between the skill of jobs and the skill of people ... Social historians have focused predominantly on the skilled divide within the manual working class and particularly on the role of apprenticed craftsmen in the development of trade unionism. There is, therefore, no shared conception of skill amongst social scientists. The concept is both multivalent and complex.

(Francis and Penn 1994, p. 223)

Yet, while recognizing these differences, we can go further than this. One analyst, for example, working from a comparison of the professional and amateur approaches to painting a room, has identified five main characteristics of skill: fluency, rapidity, automaticity, simultaneity and knowledge (Sloboda 1986). Another author presents a somewhat similar listing:

There are four criteria for the application of the term 'skill':
1   a situation of some complexity;
2   a performance that addresses the situation is deliberate and is not just a matter of chance;

3   an assessment that the performance has met the demands
    of the situation;
4   a sense that the performance was commendable.

(Barnett 1994, p. 56)

Unlike the previous listing, this formulation does not specify,
but implies, the existence of some relevant knowledge.
From these analyses we can detect some of the problems with
applying the concept. For it is not just multi-valent but multi-
level: we can use the same term to talk about an international
concert pianist and our local plumber. Not surprisingly, it is with
the latter that most concerns are raised – namely, how to increase
the skill levels of the working population in order to enable us
to better compete in the global economy.

This interest, coupled with the recognition that neither
education nor work is for life, has led to the recent concern
with developing what have been called personal transferable
skills (e.g. Bradshaw 1992, Bridges 1993). Developed in the initial
period of education, and refined through continuing education
and training, such generic skills are supposed to make workers
more flexible (see the discussion of flexible in Chapter 5), adapt-
able and able to learn. Personal transferable skills are at the heart
of the capability and enterprise initiatives, discussed in the next
section, and are also central to the competency movement, the
subject of the section after that.

Before leaving the concept of skill, however, we should recognize that, like knowledge and other concepts, it is both socially
constructed and a political term. The degree to which a performance is regarded as commendable, to use Barnett's words, is
a matter of perception, and that perception crucially depends
upon status: the status accorded to the performer and the performance, and the status of the person making the judgement.
Hence, the concert pianist is likely to be regarded by most people
as more skilful than your local plumber.

Since issues of power and status are involved, skill also has
a crucial gender component: 'the classification of women's jobs
as unskilled and men's jobs as skilled or semi-skilled frequently
bears little relation to the actual amount of training or ability
required for them. Skill definitions are saturated with sexual
bias' (Phillips and Taylor 1986, p. 55).

These views are linked to perceptions of paid and unpaid
work, and to the varied interpretations of career (Sinclair 1991;

see the section on career in Chapter 4). There are clear implications here for changing patterns of work: 'Feminisation of a particular occupation or profession is seen to have the effect of deskilling it' (Rees 1992, p. 17). School-teaching, for example, particularly at primary level, might be seen as an illustrative case of this process in operation.

CAPABILITY AND ENTERPRISE

Capability and enterprise are two concepts that came to prominence in the United Kingdom in the 1980s and 1990s. They do, however, have a longer history and more general meanings, and have also been similarly applied to education and training in other countries (e.g. Bennett and McCoshan 1993, Shuttleworth 1993). While they could not be said to be as influential now as they were a decade ago, their development and application is still of interest, as it tells us much about the use of concepts for politics and policy.

While there are similarities between these two concepts, there were key differences in their promotion and in the level of resourcing behind them. Capability was a slogan launched by the Royal Society of Arts, a body concerned to bring together educators and industrialists, and advance their joint interests. Enterprise, on the other hand, was one of the key concepts underlying the thinking of the Conservative governments of the period, and heavily funded through the Manpower Services Commission and its successor bodies (Barnett 1994, Burgess 1986). Whether either concept has had a lasting impact of itself (as opposed, that is, to contributing to underlying trends) on the education and training landscape would be a matter for debate.

It was a characteristic of both of these initiatives that neither of the promoting bodies saw a pressing need to define what they were talking about, or seeking to encourage, with any precision. It was left, at least initially, to those seeking funding or support through the initiatives to interpret what the promoters were after. This was sometimes excused on the grounds of the difficulty of definition:

> Capability does not lend itself to detailed definition. It is easier to recognise it than to measure it with any precision. It is an integration of confidence in one's knowledge, skills, self-esteem and values . . . Capable people have confidence in their

ability to (1) take effective and appropriate action, (2) explain what they are about, (3) live and work effectively with others, and (4) continue to learn from their experiences, both as individuals and in association with others, in a diverse and changing society.

(Stephenson 1992, pp. 1–2)

As this quotation indicates, however, the early reluctance to be precise was soon supplanted by a quite detailed, though not necessarily particularly helpful, formulation. What is given here is a very general definition of some of the desirable qualities of fellow workers or citizens. There are not many hints as to what a 'capability curriculum' might look like, nor as to how it might differ from learning activities lacking that conceptual heading.

This lack of precision did not, however, prevent a broad mixture of educators and industrialists from endorsing the Education for Capability movement. Nor did it stop the officers of that movement from visiting and recognizing courses or programmes as developing capability in their students. Not surprisingly, these processes themselves led to the identification of some common features. Thus, the leaders of the Higher Education for Capability offshoot of the movement came to recognize four themes:

- reviewing and building upon previous experience, knowledge and skills;
- preparing plans and negotiating approvals;
- active and interactive learning;
- the assessment of performance according to agreed learning outcomes.

(Stephenson and Weil 1992)

The enterprise initiative may be seen to have been more narrowly focused than the capability movement. Its concern was with the development of just work, rather than work and life skills. The Conservative governments of the 1980s and 1990s were responsible for launching and funding a whole raft of enterprise schemes. These covered the themes of employment and unemployment, education and training. They ranged in their targets across the lifespan from schoolchildren to older adults, though youths were the key target. Among these schemes were, for example, the Technical and Vocational Education Initiative, the Enterprise Allowance Scheme, Enterprise in Higher Education,

Enterprise Awareness in Teacher Education and even Evangelical Enterprise (MacDonald and Coffield 1991).

Enterprise in Higher Education (EHE), to take just one example, was launched in 1987, and promised one million pounds each to higher education institutions which were prepared to embed enterprise throughout their curricula. As in the case of the capability movement, enterprise was not initially defined (Burke 1991), but it was clearly implicit that only applications endorsing the Manpower Services Commission's particular view of enterprise would receive funding. Within a year of the launch, the sponsors, now renamed as the Training Agency, had become more explicit:

> As well as being qualified in a particular discipline, students who have attended a course which includes enterprise will:
> * have a positive attitude towards enterprise activity;
> * have developed personal transferable enterprise skills;
> * be better informed about employment opportunities, aims and challenges and make better career choices;
> * be better prepared to contribute to and to take responsibility in their professional and working lives.
>
> (Training Agency 1989, p. 5)

Tensions can be identified within this statement between the development of 'skills' and the inculcation of 'attitudes' (as they similarly can be in the reference to values in the capability definition quoted). Some have seen this as tantamount to suggesting a process of indoctrination to make students more favourably disposed towards enterprise. The vocational focus was transparently obvious, and most EHE programmes duly involved local employers in the planning, delivery and even assessment of courses, and developed 'realistic' project work and placement schemes. Bids for funding identified a limited range of personal transferable skills that would be developed in students, typically including problem-solving, groupwork and presentational skills.

With a further year's experience of the programme, the Training Agency was ready to reflect back to its educational audience the implicit and explicit meanings of the concept that they had identified:

> there are many definitions of 'enterprise'. Definitions may focus on:

- Entrepreneurship: the qualities and skills which enable people to succeed in business enterprises
- Personal effectiveness: the qualities and skills possessed by the resourceful individual
- Transferable skills: the generic capabilities which allow people to succeed in a wide range of different tasks and jobs.

(Training Agency 1990, p. 5)

A reasoned assessment of the Enterprise in Higher Education initiative would be that it has had at best modest success, in terms of getting academics to think about and implement both curriculum and staff development (Becher 1994, Her Majesty's Inspectors 1992). Both the concept and its implementation were heavily criticized. For some this critique was based on what was seen as unwarranted government interference, for others on a challenge to the traditions of liberal education, and for still others on the perceived inability of employers to make effective use of recruits with enterprise skills (Bailey 1992, Foreman-Peck 1993, Tasker and Packham 1994).

More generally, the whole movement for embedding industrial values within education, of which the capability and enterprise schemes can be seen as parts, has been ably deconstructed by Coffield:

> we are not dealing with a tightly defined, agreed and unitary concept but with a 'farrago' of hurrah words like 'creativity', 'initiative' and 'leadership' ... some notions which are central to most definitions of enterprise, problem-solving for instance, have been taken from psychology and then simplified, decontextualised and invested with a significance and power which few psychologists would be prepared to support ... the potential terms of reference of words like 'capability' or 'skills' (or 'enterprise') are so wide that to call someone 'capable' or 'skilful' (or 'enterprising') without specific context is meaningless ... enterprise tends to be viewed as an individual attribute and both structural factors and local economic conditions are ignored ... where is the independent and convincing evidence of the success of enterprise education or enterprise initiatives?

(Coffield 1990, pp. 67–8)

The problem with capability and enterprise is not just that they are so self-evidently, in the applications discussed here, transient buzz-words, lacking in hard, analytical credibility; but in the assumptions that they make about educators and trainers, their employers and their clients. These groups are seen simultaneously as sharing common aims and being highly malleable. That the commonality of their aims might be only apparent at a general and simplistic level, disguising an underlying and possibly healthy diversity of practice, is not seen as important, provided that they can be persuaded or cajoled into endorsing and operating common approaches.

The capability and enterprise movements may thus be seen as expressions of a fundamental lack of trust in British education and training institutions and providers. The drive towards competency-based education and training, the subject of the next section, may be viewed in a similar fashion, though it differs in terms of both its overall scope and the degree of control imposed. In that sense, it represents a further development of the desire to centralize influence and control over a recalcitrant educational service.

COMPETENCE

Like many changes in social policy, the idea of competency-based education and training was transferred to Britain from the USA (Dolowitz *et al.* 2000). The spur for its application was the perceived lack of relevance of existing vocational provision and the need to compete better with other economies (see the section on the Globalization of Adult Education and Training in Chapter 2):

> One of the growing concerns amongst employers has been that much of the provision of VET [vocational education and training] was not seen as being directly relevant to the needs of employment . . . it was considered that VET tended to be 'educationally' oriented both in content and the values which are implicit in its delivery. It has tended to concentrate on the acquisition of knowledge and theory while neglecting performance, and it is performance which essentially characterizes competence.
>
> (Jessup 1989, p. 66)

In response, the British government set up a Working Party on Vocational Qualifications, which reported in 1986. It defined its core interests in the following terms:

> A vocational qualification is a statement of competence clearly relevant to work and intended to facilitate entry into, or progression in, employment, further education and training, issued by a recognized body to an individual. This statement of competence should incorporate the assessment of:
> - skills to specified standards;
> - relevant knowledge and understanding;
> - the ability to use skills and to apply knowledge and understanding to the performance of relevant tasks.
>
> (Working Group on Vocational Qualifications 1986, p. 17)

Competence itself was defined later on in the report as 'the ability to perform a particular activity to a prescribed standard' (ibid., p. 59). This framework was quickly accepted by the government of the day, and a National Council for Vocational Qualifications (NCVQ) was established to oversee the rapid introduction of National Vocational Qualifications (NVQs), and later General National Vocational Qualifications (GNVQs), throughout education and training (Burke 1995, Hodkinson and Issitt 1995, Jessup 1991).

The introduction of a national competence-based education and training (CBET) system was welcomed in some quarters as providing a positive challenge:

> CBET has a constructive effect on some long-held assumptions about designing and assessing learning programmes ... It confronts the unthinking acceptance of institution-bound, formal, time-served programmes, and raises questions about whether traditional forms of assessment really do address the learning outcomes teachers claim to promote.
>
> (Ecclestone 1994, pp. 155–6)

These challenges included the identification of what competences actually measured, and what they did not:

> *Competence is concerned with what people can do rather than with what they know. This has several implications:*
> *firstly* if competence is concerned with doing then it must have a *context* ...

secondly competence is an *outcome*: it describes what someone can do. It does not describe the learning process which the individual has undergone . . .

thirdly in order to measure reliably someone's ability to do something, there must be clearly defined and widely accessible *standards* through which performance is measured and accredited;

fourthly competence is a measure of what someone can do *at a particular point in time.*

(Unit for the Development of Adult Continuing Education (UDACE) 1989, p. 6, original emphasis)

The issue of what UDACE referred to as 'context', and the Working Party described as 'relevant knowledge and understanding', was clearly also of critical importance. Hence it became necessary to identify not only the specific competences required and tested for, but also what became known as their 'underpinning' knowledge and understanding (Eraut 1997, Fletcher 1991, Lloyd and Cook 1993, Wolf 1995). When this was taken into account, the idea of competence could be talked of in rather broader terms, and might be seen as little removed from, or as a successor to, the concepts of capability and enterprise, discussed in the preceding section.

One of the problems with CBET, though, is that the concept of competence continues to be articulated and used in a variety of ways:

One can distinguish four different ways of conceptualising core competences:
1   Metacompetence or metacognitive skills, i.e. the intellectual skills involved in competent learning and problem solving . . .
2   Basic competences or core skills, i.e. the core body of knowledge and skills that must be learned as a foundation for all other learning . . .
3   Integrated model of competency: the ability to act within an organisation which is dependent on the holistic integration of technical, methodological, social and behavioural competences . . .
4   Organisationally embedded competency: the outcome from the interaction between skills, technical infrastructure, roles and organisational social system.

(Darmon *et al.* 1998, p. 27)

At whatever level it has been conceived, however, the concept and the policy have attracted a good deal of criticism. One of the earlier published critiques noted that:

> The idea of assessing through the use of competence statements and associated performance criteria is superficially attractive since it appears to guarantee a certain level of ability which may be expected to be transferable from the specific situation in which it was acquired. However ... the competence notion has been stretched too far ... we believe that 'competence' is the embodiment of a mechanistic, technically-oriented way of thinking which is normally inappropriate to the description of human action, or the facilitation of the training of human beings.
>
> (Ashworth and Saxton 1990, pp. 23–4)

Or, as a more recent critic has put it, rather more trenchantly: 'Competency-based standards are not so much a metaphor for technical-rationalism but more a set of tools used by technical-rationalism to disguise and make more palatable some of its operations' (Garrick 1998, p. 102). Others have attacked the policy as imprecise, confused, reductionist and applicable only to certain lower-level skills or activities: 'these aims are basic minimum, lowest common denominator ones, and leave just about everything else to be said about VET, adult and higher education' (Hyland 1994, p. 99).

These criticisms suggest a linkage between the concept of competence and higher-levels of skill and performance, reflected in the notions of professionalism (see the section on professional in Chapter 4) and expertise, which may be seen as being beyond 'mere' competence. This link is made explicit in the Dreyfus model of skill acquisition, which recognizes five successive stages: novice, advanced beginner, competent, proficient and expert (Dreyfus, Dreyfus and Athanasiou 1986). The distinction between the two concepts is spelt out in Benner's application of the Dreyfus model to nursing:

> Competence, typified by the nurse who has been on the job in the same or similar situations two to three years, develops when the nurse begins to see his or her actions in terms of long-range goals or plans of which he or she is consciously aware ... The expert performer no longer relies on an analytic

principle (rule, guideline, maxim) to connect his or her understanding of the situation to an appropriate action.
(Benner 1984, pp. 25–6, 31)

In other words, experts can perceive large and meaningful
patterns in their domains of expertise, and they have deeper
levels of understanding (Glaser and Chi 1988).

Given the level and range of criticism that has been levelled
at the competency movement, it may seem somewhat surprising
that it has been so widely adopted within education and training,
both in Britain and elsewhere:

> It is somewhat remarkable that the considerable critical
> response levelled at the competence approach in recent years
> has done little to prevent the spread of CBET into almost every
> area of contemporary educational discourse in the UK. The
> case against CBET is certainly formidable – the behaviouristic
> and reductionistic failings of the approach are well-known . . .
> but what makes the unremitting advance of CBET perhaps all
> the more remarkable is the manner in which its advocates have
> seemed able effectively to side-step theoretical censure.
>
> (Lum 1999, p. 403)

A number of possible explanations for this success may be
advanced. One is that the vocal critics of CBET are a relatively
small minority, and that most practitioners of education and
training, punch-drunk from decades of policy change and only
too aware of the weakness of their changed contractual position,
are just seeking to get on with their jobs. Another would be that
the advocates of CBET have effectively colonized the ongoing
concerns and debates of educators and trainers:

> Student-centred learning, negotiation of individual learning
> programmes, the accreditation of prior learning, the valuing of
> non-educational and training institutions as sites of learning,
> the need for guidance and counselling of learners; all of these
> now form an essential part of the discourse of competence. In
> other words, the dichotomy of 'traditional' and 'progressive'
> educational discourse is elided . . . It is precisely through its
> articulation with liberal humanist ideas that discourses of
> competence are powerful, not simply within the formal struc-
> tures of education and training, but, more important, over and
> through learners.
>
> (Usher and Edwards 1994, pp. 107–8)

QUALITY

While the focus on the quality of education and training provision has been contemporaneous with the introduction of competency-based systems, the former concern has been much more international in its scope (Craft 1994, Freedman 1987, Vroeijenstijn 1995). It can also be seen as impacting upon all levels of provision, from school through further education and university to professional and continuing education (e.g. Ashworth and Harvey 1994, Brennan, de Vries and Williams 1997, Doherty 1994a, Tovey 1994, Zuber-Skerritt and Ryan 1994).

The model for quality that has been advocated, with government support, since the 1980s has been that of the successful private company, with the mechanisms for ensuring quality in education and training being largely taken, with little adaptation, from manufacturing industry:

> We now have a plethora of custodians of quality, all of whom are at least to some extent legitimated by the Education Reform Act of 1988, the Further and Higher Education Act of 1992 as well as the White Paper with its concerns for quality and accountability. The latter, particularly, not only referred to levels of quality assurance: quality control, validation and examination, and external assessment, but also specifically mentioned quality systems – BS5750 and Total Quality Management (TQM).
>
> (Doherty 1994b, p. 3)

In addition to quality assurance, control, validation, examination and assessment, reference may also be found to quality audit, management, enhancement, circles and improvement teams (see also the discussion of human resource development in Chapter 4). As well as the British Standard BS 5750 and other national standards, there is an International Standard ISO 9000; and, within the United Kingdom, there are related schemes such as Investors in People and the Management Charter Initiative (Critten 1993). These techniques and standards have been applied throughout the public, private and voluntary sectors, and not just in the areas of education and training (see, for example, Morgan and Murgatroyd 1994).

It would not be too far-fetched to say that, in a very short space of time, a quality industry has grown up within British education and training. It is an industry with competing branches, and one that is placing an increasing bureaucratic load on those responsible for the actual delivery of education and training.

Amidst all of this activity, however, relatively little attention has been given to just what might be meant by quality, and to whether it has distinct characteristics in an educational context. It is, after all, commonplace to hear statements along the lines of 'I don't know what quality is, but I know it when I see it' (cf. the quote from Stephenson in the section on capability in this chapter). After all, quality, like standards, is a concept or principle with which it is very difficult to disagree. While this does not excuse us from our task, it is as well to recognize the difficulties and the resonances attached to words like 'quality':

> Quality, like 'freedom' or 'justice', is an elusive concept. We all have an instinctive understanding of what it means but it is difficult to articulate. Quality is also a value-laden term: it is subjectively associated with that which is good and worthwhile.
>
> (Green 1994, p. 12)

Quality is also a contested concept that embodies tensions within itself, such as those between:

- the demands of external accountability and the processes of internal improvement;
- the idea of a gold standard and of something that is 'merely' fit for its purpose;
- criterion and norm referencing (i.e. do we judge quality in terms of some absolute standard or with reference to our competitors?);
- assessment of inputs and/or outputs, or of the whole educational or training process;
- cross-disciplinary or discipline-specific demands;
- responsive or strategic approaches

(see Barnett et al. 1994).

So how can we ensure the quality of education of training?:

> There are two answers which are not necessarily incompatible with each other. The first focuses on *processes*, the second on *outcomes*. Process-based quality assurance relies on observation of teaching and learning and the activities that support

it . . . *Inspection* is the most common form of process quality assurance. Outcome-based quality assurance relies on the *assessment* of the outcomes against certain pre-agreed standards. Examination and testing are the most common forms.

(Winch and Gingell 1999, p. 197)

Ultimately, of course, it is difficult to see how anyone could ever be entirely satisfied with the quality of anything, be it an artifact or a service. We could always potentially do better. So there is no end to quality assurance and assessment. Seen in this light, the current concern with quality – like the capability, enterprise and competence movements – is in large part to do with control.

A POLITICAL BATTLEGROUND

A series of common themes can be recognized running through the discussion of the concepts that have formed the focus for this chapter. These themes can be seen in operation at a number of levels.

Thus, we can identify tensions within the concepts themselves. If we call someone skilful, capable, enterprising or competent, are we saying something banal or praiseworthy? Are these minimal or acceptable standards? How can they be measured or assessed? These tensions can even be detected, though to a lesser extent, in the concepts of knowledge and quality. If, for example, we refer to something as everyday knowledge, we may, depending upon our perspective, be dismissing it as commonplace or holding it up as of value.

Second, the interrelationships between the concepts analysed are close and complex, involving opposition and overlap. It is common to find advocates of one concept decrying another, reflecting the continuing dissonance between the core concepts of education and training. Yet it is also common to see the concepts identified defined in terms of, as well as in relation to, each other. The closer the analysis, the more skill slides into knowledge and the nearer competence comes to understanding.

Third, this conceptual battleground is also, and perhaps primarily, a political battleground. Underlying the debates reviewed here is a fundamental challenge to the professionalism of educators, trainers and their institutions. This challenge is coming from policy-makers and funders who are convinced that our vocational education and training systems have not been delivering what is required of them, to the detriment of the competitiveness of the economy. Hence we are not just dealing with concepts here, but also with slogans and their supporting ideologies.

FURTHER READING

Barnett, R (1994) *The Limits of Competence: knowledge, higher education and society*. Buckingham, Open University Press.
    Careful unpacking of many of the conceptual issues surrounding the use of the terms knowledge and competence, with particular reference to higher education.
Coffield, F (1990) 'From the decade of enterprise culture to the decade of TECs'. *British Journal of Education and Work*, 4, 1, pp. 59–78.
    Comprehensive discussion and critique of the British Conservative government's education and training policies during the 1980s.
Doherty, G (ed.) (1994) *Developing Quality Systems in Education*. London, Routledge.
    Useful accounts of the impact of the quality debate at different educational levels.
Kelly, A (1999) *The Curriculum: theory and practice*. London, Paul Chapman, fourth edition.
    Highly regarded and much used text.
Nowotny, H, Scott, P and Gibbons, M (2001) *Re-thinking Science: knowledge and the public in an age of uncertainty*. Cambridge, Polity Press.
    Influential account of the changing nature of knowledge and its implications.

Chapter 7

Structural Concepts

INPUT, EXPERIENCE AND OUTPUT

This chapter examines a series of concepts that have to do with the structure, volume and experience of adult education and training. Collectively, these concepts are concerned with a group of important issues:

- inclusion within, and exclusion from, provision;
- how what is offered is organized; and
- what benefits and disbenefits stem from participation.

In other words, the content and the ordering of the discussion in this chapter can be seen to parallel the processes of education, learning and training themselves; moving from input through experience to output.

Clearly, there are linkages between this chapter and the preceding two, which are concerned with learning and curricular concepts. While this chapter focuses on the overall organization of the learning experience, Chapter 5, on learning concepts, looks at some of the models which have been applied to adult education and training. Chapter 6, on curricular concepts, examines some of the issues or ideas that have been seen to underlie approaches to education and learning. As this synopsis itself indicates, however, the distinctions between the kinds of concepts discussed in these three chapters are relatively fine ones, and they could, of course, have been organized rather differently.

The first six of the seven concepts analysed in this chapter have been grouped in three pairs: access and participation, accreditation and modularization, and success and dropout. The first pair has to do with entry to the learning experience, both at the individual level and in overall terms. The second two are concerned with different ways of organizing or recognizing the learning experience to which entry has been gained or granted. And the third pair relates to the results of the learning experience, and how these may be assessed or evaluated. The final concept discussed, social inclusion, is presented as a broader, more contemporary and highly politicized way of considering the issues involved in access and participation.

ACCESS AND PARTICIPATION

> St Matthew's law of access and participation:
>> Unto everyone that hath shall be given, and he shall have abundance: but from him that hath not shall be taken away even that which he hath (Gospel according to St Matthew, King James version, 25, 29).
>
> (Tight 1998a, p. 258)

Access and participation emerged as major policy issues in post-school education, both in the United Kingdom (see, for example, Parry and Wake 1990, Smithers and Robinson 1989) and world-wide (Davies 1995, Halsey 1992) in the 1980s and 1990s. More recently, policy discussion of these issues has been incorporated within the debate on social inclusion (a concept examined later in this chapter).

While the concept of access has undeniable political resonance, whether the subject is access to education, health care, social security or whatever, the idea of participation may seem to be more neutral and thus straightforward:

> In its most widely accepted sense, 'participation' implies taking part in some definite, observable activity. Hence, so far as adult learning is concerned, the linkage between participation and formal educational or training 'courses'. In such cases, participation can readily be checked: the presence of individuals on courses may be observed, and there is frequently some end product in the form of an attendance certificate or qualification.
>
> (Tight 1998c, p. 115)

Seen in this way, the individual adult is either a participant – i.e. he or she engages in education, learning, training or whatever activity is of interest – or a non-participant. This status may change from time to time, but at any one point should be clear. In practice, however, participation may not be so clear-cut, not only because of the rather amorphous nature of activities such as learning, but also because the extent of individual commitment may vary. Thus, participation can be viewed as a continuous rather than a dichotomous variable (Cookson 1986).

For most institutional providers of education and training, and their funders, the concept tends to be viewed as relatively unproblematic. For example, the Organization for Economic Cooperation and Development (OECD) once defined participation in the following terms: 'to qualify as a participant an adult should attend a sequence of meetings or complete a cycle of exercises' (OECD 1977, p. 11). However, this kind of definition immediately raises a whole series of practical and detailed questions: how many meetings and how many exercises? Does the learner have to be present throughout the meetings, and be active while present, to qualify as a participant? Do they have to successfully complete all of the exercises? These questions are not trivial. They underlie many of the methodologies which funding bodies use to determine the allocation of resources to educational institutions. They also necessitate a good deal of time-consuming, bureaucratic activity in order to produce satisfactory responses. The quality of these responses will, of course, as with any human activity, be variable, partly because of the quality and precision of the definitions on which they are based.

Given these reservations, we should be careful in interpreting statistics on participation in adult education and training (Tight 1998c; see also the discussion in the section on learning in Chapter 1). Despite these difficulties, however, a considerable amount of research in this area has focused on the collection of data, through surveys of adult participation (and non-participation) in education and training at national, local or institutional level. Much effort has also been expended upon attempts to explain the data collected, and the patterns found in or suggested by it. Participation surveys typically involve the administration of a large number of questionnaires or structured interviews to a selected sample or defined group of the general adult population at a specific time (e.g. Beinart and Smith 1997, Gallie and White 1993, Sargant et al. 1997). Longitudinal studies, which trace adults' participation over a period of time, are much less common (e.g. Banks et al. 1992, Jenson, Gray and Sime 1991).

Such surveys normally collect information on a wide variety of individual characteristics that might affect participation or non-participation in education and training, including social, economic and demographic factors. They may also record details of any educational or training courses that their respondents are following, and of other learning activities in which they are engaged. The large quantitative data sets that result from these surveys then readily lend themselves to cross-tabulation or correlation, as well as to more complex multivariate analyses.

Participation surveys provide a major source of data for understanding why adults involve themselves in learning, the routes they take through education and training, their experience along the way, and the effects which this has upon them (Courtney 1992, Maguire, Maguire and Felstead 1993, McGivney 1990). They typically show, for example, a strong relationship between adult participation and previous educational experience and qualifications, and varied linkages between the kinds of learning activities engaged in and the sex and age of the participant (Tight 1995). To date, however, such studies have not led to the development of a comprehensive and successful theory that can be used to explain why adults engage in learning activities, and how this relates to their work and other roles. To gain this kind of understanding, more detailed, more narrowly focused, longitudinal and qualitative methods of research would seem to be required.

The concept of access can be seen as offering one means for analysing the broad question of participation. Access has to do with who gets educational or training opportunities and who does not. This analysis operates at both the individual level and in overall terms, when gender, class, wealth, race, disability and other social characteristics may be seen as of key importance. Thus, participation surveys consistently demonstrate that access to higher status forms of education and training is granted disproportionately to white, middle-class and able-bodied men.

Adult education may in itself be seen as expressing an ideology of needs, access and provision (Griffin 1983). In other words, it has, and has always had, an essential concern with issues of access. In the British context, however, and in many other industrialized countries, the impact of the idea of access has arguably been felt most keenly during the last two decades, and most particularly in the sectors of further and higher education. The remainder of this section will consider the example of higher education in a little more detail, where policies on access and, more recently, widening participation (Thomas 2001), have been seen by government as one means of influencing the profiles and practices of higher education institutions.

There is an important distinction to be drawn here between the broad idea of access and the much more specific manifestation of access courses. Access courses may be defined as courses designed for mature students seeking entry to further or higher education, which offer an alternative to established examination systems designed for adolescents. While they have been of increasing importance, they are far from being the only methods of enabling adult access to further and higher education.

Those within the access course movement may be seen as working in a long established 'tradition', sharing many of the beliefs and practices of some older forms of adult education (see the section on adult and continuing in Chapter 3). Their concern is chiefly with extending educational participation to those who would otherwise be excluded:

> The proponents of access courses themselves seem almost universally to belong to the *social engineering* approach to admissions. It is a radical movement in the sense that it sees education as a means by which whole social groups can improve their social, economic and political positions within British society. It is also radical in an educational sense. The social groups which represent the primary clients of Access courses are seen to have been 'failed' by the conventional educational system. The Access-course movement is founded on a rejection of such failure and of the criteria which have defined it.
>
> (Brennan 1989, p. 57, original emphasis)

The nationwide development of access courses to provide a 'third route' (alongside the existing routes through academic and vocational qualifications) into higher education offers a rather standardized solution to this perceived problem. While it is undeniable that they have enabled many individuals to pursue their education further than they might otherwise have been able to do, access courses arguably have yet to have a major impact upon the social make-up or assumptions of higher education (Burke 2002, Halsey 1993).

Access to and through further and higher education for adult students lacking the conventional entry qualifications is possible by many other means than access courses (Tight 1993). These include access through examination or assessment, through liberal adult education provision, through the assessment of prior learning, through probationary enrolment, and through open entry schemes (see the discussions of open and experiential learning in Chapter 5, and of accreditation later in this chapter). Most institutions of further and higher education, in Britain and many other countries, currently use one or more of these methods, sometimes in combination. The effect of equating access narrowly with access courses, and ignoring these other, long-standing alternatives, may actually be a reduction in overall accessibility and participation (Wright 1991). It would also deny the fuller meaning of the term access.

ACCREDITATION AND MODULARIZATION

The notion that a market in credits empowers the learner has become an orthodoxy in the formal education system.

(Elliott 1999, p. 34)

The twin concepts of modularization and accreditation are central to many contemporary debates about adult education and training. They also encapsulate two key issues in the structuring of learning experiences by educational and other institutions:

• How should the learning experience be ordered?
• How should the learning experience be assessed?

While modularization is now the standard response to the first of these questions (Higher Education Quality Council 1996), so the accreditation of modules, or their equivalents, represents at least a partial answer to the second.

At the heart of the concept of modularization is the idea that educational or training provision should be organized in terms of a series of modules:

A *module* or course unit is a self-contained block or unit of study which has a standard size or some method of agreeing a standard value ... A *course* comprises the range of units of study available to students leading to a particular award ... A *programme of studies* is an individual student's pathway through the course.

(Ram 1989, p. 3)

There is not, however, just one standard agreed scheme of modularization. Modular systems are commonly specific to groups of institutions, individual institutions, departments or even courses. This may present problems if students wish to transfer between courses and/or institutions, with issues of equivalence frequently arising.

Different providers have also adopted modular schemes with varying degrees of enthusiasm. At one extreme is the simple recasting of an existing course, or set of courses, in a modular format, with no other changes and hence no increased flexibility for the student. Towards the other extreme are systems which modularize the whole of an institution's provision, breaking down boundaries between subjects and courses, and enabling individual students to create their own programmes of study (Squires 1986). Such systems may also allow students to earn modules through extended project work or the accreditation of prior learning (see also the section on experiential in Chapter 5).

There is nothing particularly new about the idea of modularization. It has been common practice for many years in American colleges and universities, was adopted by the British Open University from its inception in 1969, and was used by the University of London before then. Nevertheless:

> Modularity is fashionable. The reasons are well-rehearsed – new clients with new needs and mixed modes of study, customer choice, credit frameworks, blurring boundaries between academic disciplines, new integrations between 'academic' and 'vocational' programmes, the pressure of Assessment of Prior Experiential Learning (APEL) and National Vocational Qualifications (NVQs) – and a claimed cost-effectiveness. The curricular case for well-designed modular programmes is also well-rehearsed – student choice, learner autonomy, flexibility for individual student circumstances, adaptability to new modes of learning and assessment, speed of response to external pressures and agencies, openness to new kinds of knowledge and new connections. As with all things, however, its potential strengths are its possible weaknesses. Poorly designed modular programmes are vulnerable to intellectual incoherence, to problems with continuity and progression of learning, to loss of student identity and to excessive bureaucracy.
>
> (Walker 1994, pp. 24–5)

The widespread adoption of modularization by adult education and training providers in the United Kingdom and other countries may be linked to external pressures to increase participation rates and flexibility, while simultaneously reducing unit costs. Modular schemes may appear, at least in principle, to offer significant advantages to both providers and participants.

Thus, they may offer savings to an institution where courses share some of the same modules, or where available spare places can be filled with students from other courses. However, such savings come at some cost in terms of increased administration and class sizes, reduced individual attention to students and staff stress. Similarly, while modularization may offer more choice in terms of course contents to students, this can only be realized if the restrictions on modular combinations caused by timetabling or previous study requirements are minimized (Watson *et al.* 1989). In many cases, therefore, the benefits and impacts of modularization for students and staff may be limited (Morris 2000).

A more fundamental objection to modularization stems from concerns about the organization of knowledge and loss of expert control (see also the discussion of knowledge in Chapter 6). Many professional educators and trainers, understandably, believe that they have a far better understanding of what learners need, and of what is required in a course, than the learners themselves. While this need not preclude some flexibility and individualization of the curriculum, it suggests that, at the very least, the overall structure of the learning experience, and the pathways through it, should remain under the direct control of the educator or trainer.

From this perspective, the more flexible or open systems of modularization may be criticized as overly reductionist and lacking in coherence. After all, where the learner has a largely free choice over which combination of modules to study – often referred to as the 'cafeteria' approach – where does the responsibility lie for ensuring that they are able to make some overall sense of their programme of study? With the learners themselves, perhaps with some oversight? There is a risk here that the role of the educator or trainer is reduced to simply delivering more or less arbitrary 'chunks' of learning.

Similar reservations and criticisms have been made regarding the extension of accreditation throughout the education and training system. Accreditation has to do with the recognition of what learners have learned, and has always been a major role of educators and trainers. In essence, it may be argued that the only distinct role of educational bodies – as opposed to, for example, business or community organizations – remains their ability to grant individuals qualifications or awards which have national and international standing.

The conventional approach has long been that such accreditation relates largely or exclusively to learning that has taken place under supervised conditions within a recognized educational or training institution. The current interest in accreditation has more to do, however, with recognizing the worth of learning wherever it has taken place, and however it was gained. Accreditation in this sense is not, though, a recent innovation. Like many developments in education and training, it has come to the United Kingdom, in the last decade or so, from the United States. The original philosophy can, however, be traced back to Britain, where organizations like the University of London were behind much pioneering work (Bell and Tight 1993).

Like other policies targeted at vocational education and training (see the discussion of competence in Chapter 6), the current impetus behind the development of accreditation in Britain has much to do with the perception of the workforce as under-skilled and under-qualified. The wider use of accreditation systems is seen as one practical response. It allows the recognition of much existing but uncredited learning, and, perhaps more significantly, the development of more flexible means for encouraging future learning (see the discussion of flexible in Chapter 5). Thus learning may be undertaken on-the-job, or in one's spare time, rather than requiring costly release from work. Indeed, some have gone so far as to argue for the creation of a 'credit culture' (Higher Education Quality Council 1994).

The accreditation movement has major implications, of course, for the roles of educators, trainers and the organizations for whom they work. They may become increasingly concerned not just with the accreditation of learners who have followed their own courses, but with the accreditation of any learning in their areas of expertise, whether they have been responsible for it or not. Such accredited learning may then be accepted as part of a larger programme of study, part of which may be undertaken within the accrediting institution itself.

Many institutions and providers have become increasingly interested in systems for the accreditation of prior learning, and there have been a number of publications produced that aim to guide educators or trainers through the relevant processes (e.g. Challis 1993, Simosko 1991). These processes would typically include the identification and selection of relevant learning, the demonstration of its validity, the matching of learning outcomes, the assessment of the evidence presented and then, if satisfactory, its accreditation. Clearly, these processes could be enlightening, but also potentially very time-consuming, both for the individual and the institution concerned. In some cases, then, it might well be argued that it would be easier, and perhaps cheaper, to under-take a course for credit rather than have prior learning accredited.

The critique of the accreditation movement goes deeper than this: there are other practical and educational objections. As with modularization, in the United Kingdom there is no one standard and nationally recognized credit system, though the work of the National Council for Vocational Qualifications (now part of the Qualifications and Curriculum Authority) has moved matters in this direction. From an educational point of view, the wish to accredit as much learning as possible can be seen as both limiting and off-putting. It runs counter to the values espoused in the idea of liberal education (see the discussion in Chapter 1). Thus, it has been argued that 'credit levels construct the learner and label and define experience' (Avis 1991, p. 40).

Is the only, or the over-riding, value of learning to be seen in the number and level of credit points it earns for the learner? If so, this may influence not just how we learn but what we learn, in our desire to gain those credits as quickly, easily and cheaply as possible. For many adults, such an approach would be both meaningless and stultifying. In an increasingly competitive and uncertain working environment, accreditation for vocational purposes may be more and more essential. Yet, one of the chief delights of learning undertaken for other purposes, or for no particular purpose at all, remains the lack of pressure to engage with assessment and accreditation in any form.

SUCCESS AND DROPOUT

Most studies of adult education and training have focused either on the characteristics of the learners or on the nature of the learning opportunities made available to them. Less attention has been given to the success or otherwise of the learning experience, and the reasons for this, despite continuing concerns about the numbers of adults who fail to complete (or drop out from) courses or programmes. The whole area of evaluation has too often been regarded as of limited interest (Edwards 1991, Harris and Bell 1990), though this is changing in the light of current concerns with quality (see the section on quality in Chapter 6).

Of course, assessing the relative success or failure of adult education or training is not a straightforward exercise. It will normally not be adequate to make a once and for all judgement at the end of a given learning experience. Success and failure are relevant concepts before and at the point of entry, during the learning experience, at its completion, and afterwards. We also have to recognize that our individual perspectives on the success or failure of a learning experience – whether as learners, teachers or providers – will vary over time, so that we may, for example, only come to appreciate its value years afterwards.

Studies of the success of actual learning experiences, as they are taking place, have focused on how learners' expectations compare with the reality of their courses or programmes. Many of these studies have looked at mature students in higher education, often comparing their experiences with those of younger students (Metcalf 1993, Roberts, Higgins and Lloyd 1992). They have frequently identified a dissonance between the over-expectations of learners and their actual experiences, which can lead to considerable disappointment (Weil 1986). While some dissonance is to be expected, it is obviously in the interests of those concerned to find ways of minimizing and responding to such problems.

The relative success of a formal learning experience, once completed, is most commonly and easily assessed through measuring performance in some kind of examination or test. This remains the normal approach in both conventional and competence-based forms of education and training, whether continuous, repeated or single forms of assessment are used (e.g. Messick 1999, Palomba and Banta 1999). As with studies of progress on course, much attention here has been devoted to how the performance of adults compares with that of younger age groups. Thus, for example, studies of the progress and performance of adult students in higher education have tended to show that adults, and those with 'non-traditional' entry qualifications, are, on average, as successful in their studies as younger students (Molloy and Carroll 1992, Smithers and Griffin 1986).

It is much more difficult, of course, to assess the benefits or disadvantages of learning experiences in broader as well as non-quantitative terms. Where courses or programmes do not involve formal testing or examination, evaluation is perhaps even more important, but all too often is carried out only in a fairly superficial manner. More detailed and longer-term studies are needed to identify the changes in attitudes, identity, quality of life and values which education, in its fullest sense, is intended to achieve (Pascarella and Terenzini 1991). Thus, a fifty year, quantitative study of a cohort of Swedish men concluded that:

> As the direct effects of adult education on occupational status increase over time, the total effects of the former on earnings mediated by occupational status also increase with age . . . In general, participants in adult education regard their lives as more worthwhile, full, rich and interesting than those who do not take part.

> (Tuijnman 1989, p. 4)

Shorter term and cross-sectional studies of the effects of education and training specifically on employment are more common (see, for example, Boys and Kirkland 1988, Brown and Webb 1990). The recent growth of interest in adult learning routes, focusing on how adults link learning experiences together, and relate them to employment and other activities, is also relevant here (McGivney 1992, 1993).

Studies of the success of learning experiences may be related to general studies of participation. Conversely, an interest in the issues of failure and/or dropout may be related to the idea of non-participation. Examining the voluntary or forced exclusion of many from access to learning opportunities, and the reasons for this, provides an inverse view to surveys of who participates (see, for example, McGivney 1990, and the section on access and participation earlier in this chapter).

So far as adult education and training are concerned, it has to be said that a large, and probably disproportionate, proportion of the effort that has been expended on measuring and understanding success or failure has been devoted to the issue of dropout (e.g. McGivney 1996, Peelo and Wareham 2002, Yorke 1999). It has long been recognized, of course, that many adults who begin a programme or course of study do not complete it, and attitudes towards this have varied from the concerned to the cavalier. These variations are somewhat reflected in the different terms used to label dropout, which also include the prosaic 'non-completion', the rather stronger 'retention' and the vigorous 'attrition'.

Naturally, dropout causes concern amongst many educators and trainers. Yet it may have positive as well as negative causes and consequences. Thus, learners may leave a course because they judge that their learning needs have been satisfied, or because they have identified another course better able to satisfy them. In such cases, it is not unreasonable to regard dropout as representing a success, from the individual's if not the provider's point of view. Learners may also, and perhaps most commonly, discontinue for reasons that have little to do with the learning experience itself, but relate to other demands on their time and resources, such as employment and family.

Educators and trainers, and the institutions that employ them, are understandably keen to be able to predict, with a reasonable degree of accuracy, whether adults starting a course will complete or dropout. After all, dropout may have financial consequences for providers, as well as being disruptive for other learners and their teachers or trainers. Interestingly, while British studies of dropout have tended to draw up lists of indicators (e.g. Bourner et al. 1991, Woodley and Parlett 1983), the American literature has been more explicitly concerned with the development and testing of explanatory theory (e.g. Cabrera et al. 1992, Tinto 1987). Indeed, this may be said to be one of most theorized areas of educational study.

SOCIAL INCLUSION

In the UK the concept of social exclusion came to the fore with the setting up by the government in 1997 of the inter-departmental Social Exclusion Unit.

(Percy-Smith 2000, p. 2)

Social inclusion, and its contrary twin social exclusion, arrived in British policy debate with the victory of the Labour Party in

1997, though the concept had previously been applied within Europe. It is a broadly applied concept, covering much socio-economic territory (Lister 2000), and has clear connections to other contemporary concepts much loved of politicians, such as lifelong learning, the learning society and social capital (see Chapters 2 and 4). In the context of adult education and training, social inclusion can be seen as both a successor to the earlier concerns with increasing access and widening participation (discussed earlier in this chapter), and as a focusing of this concern to make explicit the links to economic success and social cohesion (Perraton 2000).

As with most concepts, however, what social inclusion means and how it is applied is contested. Thus, Levitas identifies three main and competing discourses:

> In practice ... social exclusion is embedded in different discourses ... Three discourses are identified here: a redistributionist discourse (RED) developed in British critical social policy, whose prime concern is with poverty; a moral underclass discourse (MUD) which centres on the moral and behavioural delinquency of the excluded themselves; and a social integrationist discourse (SID) whose central focus is on paid work. They differ in how they characterize the boundary, and thus what defines people as insiders or outsiders, and how inclusion can be brought about. RED broadens out from its concern with poverty into a critique of inequality, and contrasts exclusion with a version of citizenship which calls for substantial redistribution of power and wealth. MUD is a gendered discourse with many forerunners, whose demons are criminally-inclined, unemployable young men and sexually and socially irresponsible young mothers, for whom paid work is necessary as a means of social discipline, but whose (self-)exclusion, and thus potential inclusion, is moral and cultural. SID focuses more narrowly on unemployment and economic inactivity, pursuing social integration or social cohesion primarily through inclusion in paid work.
>
> (Levitas 1998, pp. 7–8)

Any follower of contemporary political debate should immediately be able to recognize echoes and applications of these discourses. The contested nature of the concept is, though, one of its strengths:

Social exclusion is a powerful concept, not because of its analytical clarity which is conspicuously lacking, but because of its flexibility. At an individual level, it mobilizes personal fears of being excluded or left out, which reach back into childhood as well as having immediate reference. At a political level, it has broad appeal, both to those who value increased participation and those who seek greater social control. Crucially, social exclusion facilitates a shift between the different discourses in which it is embedded, so that the contested meaning of social exclusion now lies at the heart of political debate.

(ibid., p. 178)

Another of the strengths of the concept, as with other concepts discussed in this book – see, for example, the discussion of community in Chapter 3 and of open learning in Chapter 5 – is its apparent simplicity and thus broad appeal:

The intuitive core of the idea of inclusion looks simple enough. It is the idea that every member of society should participate fully in it. The social ideal that inclusion expresses is an ideal of common membership: no one is denied access to activities and practices that are central in the life of society.

(Gray 2000, p. 23)

As with all popular and all-embracing concepts, however, there are difficulties. One of these is the way in which blame is effectively placed on the socially excluded, who are expected, and assumed to be readily able, to change their ways and become socially included (cf. the discussion of lifelong learning policies in Chapter 2: Tight 1998b). In other words:

the inclusion/exclusion debate defines the problem of poverty and lack of access to social and economic resources as being about the dysfunction of particular groups in those communities. The solution offered in this model is for these people to adjust to a taken-for-granted middle-class norm of behaviour, such as retraining, to enable integration.

(Stuart 2000, p. 27)

The practicalities of social inclusion policies must, therefore, be questionable. Changing peoples' 'taken-for-granted norms of behaviour' is a very difficult and long-term process. Hence the rejection of social inclusion as a viable concept by some, who argue that it is either simply unachievable or ignores the inevitability of continuing social exclusion for some:

> What is interesting about social inclusion is that it is a concept that is both global and consensual. Like community education and lifelong learning, it is difficult to be against it ... by contrast ... we question it as a social policy goal for education and the latter's capacity to 'solve' social 'problems'... there can be no social inclusion unless there is also social exclusion. The elimination of social exclusion as a practical activity is unachievable ... Moreover, seeking to promote social inclusion heightens awareness of difference and social exclusion.
>
> (Edwards, Armstrong and Miller 2001, pp. 418–19, 426)

POLICY AND RESEARCH

The discussion in this chapter reflects and reinforces many of the general issues already noted and commented upon earlier in the book. This is apparent, for example, when we consider alternative interpretations of concepts, and the tensions between individual and organizational perspectives. But there are other concerns that have been particularly highlighted by the analysis presented here, though they also have more general application. Two of these concerns seem especially worthy of comment by way of conclusion: the impact of policy and the role of research.

Policy imperatives can be seen to underlie all of the concepts examined in this chapter. They provide the stimulus for encouraging increased access to, and participation in, education and training by adults; as well as, in the more modern parlance, ensuring social inclusion. They are the motivation for the widespread introduction of modularization, accreditation and other more flexible methods of structuring educational provision. And they underlie the concern with the success or failure of learners and the programmes they follow.

The position of research is also a theme that threads its way throughout this chapter. Educational researchers have been much concerned with the question of why individual adults participate or not in particular kinds of learning experience. They are also very exercised about why, given their decision to participate, adults may subsequently drop out from, or fail to successfully complete, their learning programmes.

Both of these factors have a dual influence on the use of concepts. At one level – particularly in the case of national policies, but also for influential research studies – they offer a single, unifying, but perhaps doctrinaire, view of what a concept means. When the government of the day, or one of the leading researchers in the field, states that a given concept has a specific meaning, it is difficult not to be influenced. But, at another, and perhaps more important level, policy development and research studies also offer a critique and a reinterpretation of others' usage and understanding of concepts.

FURTHER READING

Courtney, S (1992) *Why Adults Learn: towards a theory of participation in adult education*. London, Routledge.
Thorough consideration of the different approaches and theories which have been developed, so far with only partial success, to try and explain adult participation.

Edwards, R, Armstrong, P and Miller, N (2001) 'Include me out: critical readings of social exclusion, social inclusion and lifelong learning'. *International Journal of Lifelong Education*, 20, 5, pp. 417–28.
Healthy and thought-provoking critique of these linked concepts.

Higher Education Quality Council (1994) *Choosing to Change: extending access, choice and mobility in higher education*. London, HEQC.
National report which argues at length for the adoption of a credit culture in higher education.

Levitas, R (1998) *The Inclusive Society? Social exclusion and new labour*. Basingstoke, Macmillan.
Careful analysis of the application of the concept in its contemporary political setting.

Pascarella, E and Terenzini, P (1991) *How College Affects Students: findings and insights from twenty years of research*. San Francisco, CA Jossey-Bass.
Massive synthesis of hundreds of, mainly American, studies of the impact of higher education upon its participants.

Chapter 8

Conceptual Understandings

CONCEPTUAL CONCLUSIONS

The intention of this final chapter is not to substantially repeat the arguments and findings of the preceding chapters. Rather, the aim is to draw from those analyses some more general conclusions, which may usefully illuminate the use and understanding of concepts in adult education and training. Hopefully, these conclusions, in drawing upon and extending the frameworks for analysis suggested in the Introduction, will provide a broad structure that will be helpful in examining other concepts or related areas of study.

This chapter contains four relatively short sections that successively and collectively summarize a series of conclusions. The sections have been labelled conceptual relations, conceptual characteristics, conceptual analyses, and conceptual pasts and futures. As with the organization of the book as a whole, however, these sections are neither discrete nor entirely robust.

The section that follows briefly looks at the relationships between the kind of concepts we have been studying and five general themes: time, space, policy, theory and ideals. The next section examines three key characteristics shared by most, if not all, of the concepts included: tensions, competition and dimensions. The third section then reviews three ways in which many of the concepts considered may be analysed: in terms of social variables, organizational levels and educational linkages. Finally, the fourth section looks back to assess what has changed since the first edition of this book (Tight 1996) was published, and speculates a little about the future development of concepts in adult education and training.

CONCEPTUAL RELATIONS

In this section, the relationship between concepts in adult education and training and five broad themes will be considered. These five themes are not, of course, the only ones which could have been chosen for examination, but they are arguably amongst the most general in terms of application and relevance. They include two themes, time and space – i.e. the historical and comparative dimensions – that were anticipated in the Introduction. The three other themes chosen – policy, theory and ideals – have arisen from the analyses presented in the chapters that followed.

Time

All of the concepts that have been examined in this book – like all thoughts, ideas and constructs – are located in time. They all have a history. Even where this seems to be brief, there are the connections with other concepts of longer standing to be considered. There are a number of obvious implications which arise from this location in time, but it is surprising just how often these are overlooked, and how frequently individuals seem to believe that they are advocating 'new' concepts.

Because concepts are located in time, they are subject to change and development. There are few ideas that remain constant in their expression for any length of time. Looking back, we may think that we can identify 'traditions', or we may have them presented to us by others. Even these traditions, however, represent processes rather than constancies, and are subject to continual reinterpretation (see the section on tensions, traditions and dichotomies in Chapter 3).

Similarly, we can detect fashions in conceptual development and usage. Concepts have a 'sell-by date'. They may rise to prominence, be widely talked about, analysed and applied, only to sink into relative obscurity within comparatively few years (see, for example, the discussion of enterprise in Chapter 6). Or they move from the conceptual realm to become the basis of policy (e.g. the case of human capital, discussed in Chapter 4) and/or be taken as 'fact'.

These changes are not simply one way; in other words, concepts do not just rise, fall and disappear from usage. They are often reused or recycled once or more throughout their history, sometimes wittingly, at other times unconsciously (e.g. lifelong learning, discussed in Chapter 2). This may or may not involve a change in the wording of the concept, or perhaps even the complete substitution of one concept for another of essentially the same meaning (see, for example, the discussion of open in Chapter 5).

Space

Clearly, space complements time as the other obvious dimension in which to understand the location of concepts. Just as the application and meaning of concepts varies throughout history, and has its own history, so conceptual usage and understanding differs from place to place, and country to country. It has an international or comparative dimension.

These spatial variations in conceptual usage can be partly traced, of course, to differences in language and culture. Thus, as has been stressed a number of times in the text, the focus in this book has been primarily on anglophone concepts – those which have developed in the English and American systems in particular. Other linguistic and cultural traditions, such as the francophone, have produced and used rather different series of concepts, though in many cases these are analogous (see, for example, the discussion of lifelong education in Chapter 2).

Yet we live in an increasingly internationalized world (see the section on globalization in Chapter 2), and in some ways our ideas and practices are coming closer and closer together. Or, at least, our understanding of others' ideas and practices is improving. Hence, particularly with the post-war rise in the influence of a range of international organizations, many more concepts are coming to have global application and meaning.

Policy

All governments, political parties and interest groups make widespread use of concepts. Indeed, it could be said that concepts are central to politics, whether driven by ideological concerns or more pragmatic policy-making interests. Concepts offer convenient and superficially simple labels for more complex ideas, which can then be sold to voters or used to rally supporters (see, for example, the discussion of social inclusion in Chapter 7).

This is not to say that politicians or policy-makers actually create concepts themselves; this rarely seems to be the case. What tends to happen is that they adopt and adapt concepts which are available, and which appear to connect with the ideas and policies they are working with. The meaning and application of these concepts may then be changed quite radically, as in the case of continuing education (discussed in Chapter 3). A new vocabulary for presenting and analysing them may also be developed.

Where concepts are being used politically in these ways, they will tend to become the subject of much broader discussion and debate (see, for example, the examination of learning society in Chapter 2). They may then enter popular discussion, rather than being limited to academic or political circles, and be further developed as a result.

Theory

Concepts also have a close linkage with our ways of furthering our understanding of our world. They can provide a focus for research and theory development. They are used to encapsulate our ideas about what is particularly important or significant in any one area of interest (see, for example, the discussion of andragogy in Chapter 5). They offer a means to both organize and explain our concerns.

This is why it is so important for those who routinely handle concepts to have a better understanding of their meaning and application. Offering such an understanding is, of course, the fundamental purpose of this book. Without a broader and deeper view, it would be so easy to interpret concepts solely from one's own, inevitably relatively narrow, perspective.

Concepts also have an important enabling function so far as theory development and research are concerned. Labelling a set of issues or ideas as a concept (see, for example, the discussion of career in Chapter 4, or of experiential in Chapter 5) effectively legitimates, and to some extent demarcates, them as an area for investigation. This is a key way by which disciplinary knowledge develops.

Ideals

Just as concepts may be linked to ideology by way of their role in politics, so they may be connected with ideals. Ideals and ideology are closely related terms, of course, and may in practice be closely linked with each other. Here, however, the term 'ideals' is being used in a broader and less political sense, for concepts may be presented as ideals or ideal types to be aimed for, as hopeful aspirations, or even as utopias (see the section on ideals and fashions in Chapter 2).

In this sense, some concepts represent unreal and unachievable ideas (see, for example, the discussion of the learning organization in Chapter 2, and of independent and self-directed learning in Chapter 5). Their status as ideals does not necessarily mean, however, that they are of no practical value. They may offer a model or target against which progress and practice may be judged, even if it can never be totally emulated. Concepts may be a process rather than a product. As such, they can have a valid, inspirational role.

In a similar way, some concepts may encapsulate an ideal (for example, quality, discussed in Chapter 6) which is not so much unachievable as ill-defined. In such cases, the concept's role may be to stimulate concern and direct attention. A detailed and pragmatic working out of what the concept may mean in a given context and situation may then follow, which can then allow it to be better achieved in practice.

CONCEPTUAL CHARACTERISTICS

In addition to sharing varied relations with the themes of time, space, policy, theory and ideals, as just discussed, all of the concepts in adult education and training analysed in this book have other characteristics in common. These relate to the concepts themselves rather than their contexts. Three key characteristics will be briefly considered in this section: the tendency of concepts to exhibit tensions, their competitive status, and their positioning within dimensions.

Tensions

Part of the role of concepts could be said to be about the recognition and structuring of tensions between differing ideas or perspectives. These tensions exist both within and between the concepts themselves.

An example of the latter would be the varied use of cognate ideas like distance, open and flexible education, learning or training (see Chapter 5). In this case, it is not altogether clear which is the most general concept, to what extent they duplicate each other, and how best they might be seen as related. We might, for example, view distance learning as either a precursor or a part of open learning. Open and flexible learning, on the other hand, both seem equally all-encompassing, and might be seen as synonymous.

Interestingly, each of these three concepts also presupposes the existence of a paired but opposed 'shadow' concept. The term 'shadow' concept is used, since these are rarely articulated as such, or at least not to the same extent. These shadow concepts we might call respectively face-to-face, closed and inflexible education, learning or training. Some other examples of shadow concepts are suggested in Figure 8.1, and many more might be derived by speculating from this book's list of contents.

For an example of tensions within a concept, the notions of development (see Chapter 1) and success (see Chapter 7) may be used. In the case of development, there is an internal tension between personal and economic interpretations of the concept. In the case of success, there are tensions between simple completion and other possible measures, such that the concept may be interpreted in myriad and individual ways.

Distance education	Face-to-face education
Open learning	Closed learning
Flexible training	Inflexible training
Development	Stasis
Community	Conflict
Knowledge	Ignorance
Access	Exclusion

Figure 8.1 Concepts and shadow concepts

This review of tensions illustrates other common conceptual characteristics. Thus, instead of having somewhat hidden shadows, they may be set up as dichotomies. Examples include education/training and teaching/learning (see Chapter 1, and also the discussion of knowledge and skill in Chapter 6, especially Figure 6.1). In some cases, the distinctions being made may be more than two-fold: for example, the three-fold 'trichotomy' formal/nonformal/informal (discussed in Chapter 3).

Hence, while concepts perform the function of encapsulating important ideas, they are also about making divisions and distinctions (see, for example, the case of professional, discussed in Chapter 4). They have a dual role of inclusion and exclusion. From this point of view, it may be equally as useful to be able to say that something is not, for example, education, as it is to be able to confirm that it is.

Competition

The discussion of tensions within and between concepts slides naturally into recognition, in many cases, of their competitive status. Various gradations may be recognized here. Thus, there may be competitive views taken of the same concept (see, for example, the alternative views taken of open, discussed in Chapter 5).

Competition can also be seen as occurring between concepts that occupy much the same area of discussion, as in the case of experiential and self-directed (examined in Chapter 5). Or it may be that similar concepts are deliberately advanced by organizations or interests to compete with each other (e.g. the use of capability and enterprise, reviewed in Chapter 6).

In many cases, including those just instanced, such competition is a partial and temporary phenomenon. After all, the advocates of competing concepts of these kinds will tend to share much the same ideas, and favour similar responses to the same issues. After a period of more overt competition, therefore, the use of such concepts may become mutually reinforcing and supportive, such that their meaning and application may be almost indistinguishable to subsequent generations or audiences.

There are other instances, however, where the competition between concepts is more deep-rooted and thus longer lasting. The most obvious example amongst those discussed in this book is that between vocational and liberal views of education and training (discussed in Chapter 1). Here, the concepts are being used to label, advance and contest alternative perspectives of the whole field, and the debate has continued for many decades.

Dimensions

In practice, of course, the position is usually rather more complicated than that. People rarely advocate only vocational education, or only liberal education; or, if they do, they tend to be using the terms in a more general and inclusive fashion. Courses are neither wholly open nor wholly closed. Such concepts represent positions on a continuum, spectrum or dimension (see the discussion of the relations between education, learning and training in Chapter 1, and particularly Figure 1.2).

Thus, open–closed offers one dimension – and also, as already suggested, a dichotomy – for judging educational provision or learning experiences. This is a dimension on which all practical examples would be located away from the extreme poles of wholly open and wholly closed. Similarly, any example of education, learning or training is likely to mix elements of the vocational and liberal approaches.

Once we recognize the positioning of concepts along a variety of possible dimensions, it becomes easier to appreciate how they may overlap in certain areas, slide into each other, or even substitute one for the other. Thus, while in many instances it may be relatively easy to justify why we view a given example as education or learning, or as further rather than higher education (see Chapters 1 and 3); in other cases we might not be so sure. Though concepts may be about exclusion as well as inclusion, and may be presented as competitive terms or dichotomies, their boundaries are not necessarily precise, and are subject to perception, negotiation, interpretation and change.

CONCEPTUAL ANALYSES

The discussion so far, in the preceding chapters as well as in this one, has indicated a range of different ways in which concepts in adult education and training may be considered and analysed. The purpose of this section is to look at three particular ways (or groups of ways) by which conceptual analysis might be approached. These are in terms of underlying social variables, organizational levels or educational linkages. The first two of these methods were suggested in the Introduction (see the section on frameworks for analysis), while the third was prominent in Chapter 3.

Social variables

The consideration of underlying social variables – e.g. gender, race, class, age, etc. – in the analysis of any issue is at the heart of the social science approach. It is just as valid in the analysis of the use of concepts. In the case of gender, for example, we have seen how the interpretation of concepts like career and skill (discussed in Chapters 4 and 6), and indeed of any work-related concept, is rooted in our varying ideas of the roles and positions of men and women in society. A conventional view might equate work with full-time, continuing and paid employment, and thus take an implicitly male perspective. Other, broader views, building on the work of feminist authors, are, however, possible, useful and revealing.

The issue of age, to take a second example, underpins all discussion about adult education and training, at least implicitly. The very field of adult education and training itself is, after all, defined in distinction from child and/or youth education and training. Though adulthood constitutes the greater part of most of our lives, at least in the industrialized world, it is still quite possible to discuss adults as if they were a homogeneous group, and this is a tendency that has to be guarded against.

Age, or more broadly time, is, however, explicit in many of the concepts which have been examined; including, for example, development, lifelong, continuing, career and experiential (see Chapters 1, 2, 3, 4 and 5). These encapsulate the idea of changes during the adult's lifespan.

Organizational levels

Many of the concepts discussed in this book may be considered in terms of different organizational levels or statuses. The threefold categorization most commonly used has been that which recognizes the levels of the individual, the organization and the society. This typology may, however, be modified and added to.

We might think in terms of the group or the community, as well as the organization, as lying between the individual and societal levels. The descriptors local, regional, national and international (or global) could be used as an alternative classification, usefully bringing in a recognition of the role of governments and states, as well as of the comparative element.

Some of the concepts that have been reviewed relate only or chiefly to just one of these levels. Thus the learning organization refers primarily to the organizational level, while the learning society is concerned with the societal level (see Chapter 2). Other concepts can be interpreted at two levels. For example, career may be seen from the perspective of the individual or of the organization, while human capital may be interpreted at the individual or societal level (both of these concepts are discussed in Chapter 4).

In other cases, it is possible, and indeed sensible, to analyse single concepts or series of concepts at a variety of levels. The ideas of access and participation (examined in Chapter 7), for example, may each be approached from the point of view of the individual learner, of the educational or employing organization, and of society as a whole. Social inclusion, also discussed in Chapter 7, can be seen as a reformulation of the ideas of access and participation, but explicitly taking a societal or state perspective.

Alternatively, a series of concepts may enable an analysis of a linked succession of organizational levels. This is perhaps clearest in the case of the international concepts already referred to: lifelong learning, the learning organization, the learning society (explored in Chapter 2). These can be seen as articulating shared concern at, respectively, the individual, organizational and societal levels of analysis.

Educational linkages

As the discussion of age in the sub-section on social variables above has already indicated, it is difficult to proceed far in an analysis of concepts in adult education and training without referring to non-adult, that is child and youth, education and training. This is partly a question of definition, and partly a matter of linkage between these two broad areas.

There is, of course, no clear and absolute division between adult and non-adult forms of education and training. This was shown in the analysis of the terms post-compulsory, post-initial, post-secondary and post-school in Chapter 3 (see the section on the institutional framework). Adulthood cannot be defined solely in terms of age (as suggested in the section on adult in Chapter 1), and there are too many overlaps in provision and practice between adult and non-adult education and training. So there are inevitably some shared concerns that extend across the porous and indefinite boundaries we manage to recognize.

The linkages are, however, much stronger and more complex than that. Non-adult and adult forms of education and training are arranged in a sequential fashion, even if there are gaps, so that almost all of those involved as participants as adults will have also participated as children and youths. The nature of adult education and training is, therefore, largely a reaction or response to what is provided for children. It may take the form of supplementary education, intended to overcome deficiencies in child or youth learning. Or it may be progressional, building upon and extending what has already been learned (see further and higher in Chapter 3). Whichever the case, those involved in delivering or understanding adult education and training cannot afford to ignore developments in child and youth provision.

CONCEPTUAL PASTS AND FUTURES

In this final section, two tasks will be attempted. First, looking backwards, I (and here the first person intervenes for the first time since the Introduction) will reflect a little upon what has changed in the conceptual world in the half a decade or so since I wrote the first edition of this book: see also the section on 'what's new about the second edition?' in the Introduction. Second, looking forwards, I will speculate a little about the possible future development of concepts in adult education and training, at the same time reviewing what I said about this in the first edition.

First, then, what has changed since the first edition, written in late 1995 and published in 1996 (Tight 1996)? The major change seems to have been political and policy related. With the change of government in the United Kingdom in 1997, New Labour or Third Way notions have come to prominence in discussions of education and training, and similar trends can be identified in many other western, industrialized nations. Thus, the emphasis on social capital and social inclusion (see Chapters 4 and 7), both included in this edition for the first time, and the reemphasis on lifelong learning and the learning society (see Chapter 2), which, in 1995/96, seemed to be of more importance in an historical context.

Other changes, however, have been more practical or theoretical in nature. Here I would include the growth of interest in the idea of communities of practice and the increasing popularity of problem-based learning (both discussed in Chapter 5). We may also note the resurgence of interest in the nature of knowledge, evidenced both in the concept of knowledge management (discussed in the section on the learning organization in Chapter 2) and in the debate about types or modes of knowledge (see Chapter 6).

By implication, however, not much has changed since the first edition of the book was produced. Indeed, all of the concepts discussed then, with the sole exception of recurrent education (now subsumed by lifelong education and rarely mentioned), are still included in this edition. However, it is possible to identify some concepts that have declined in popularity. These would include:

- the idea of continuing education (see Chapter 3), now overrun by the more contemporary notion of lifelong education (Chapter 2);
- the concepts of andragogy and conscientization (see Chapter 5), which may now be seen as part of the history of adult education and training; and
- the notions of capability and enterprise (see Chapter 6), which now sound like last decade's slogans, even if much of their content is still contained in more contemporary labels.

Second, what of the future? In the first edition of this book (p. 154), I stated that I would expect many of the following conceptual developments to take place in the future:

1 A continuing recycling, reinterpretation and renaming of many existing concepts. A fairly safe prediction to make, but it has been borne out and I would expect it to continue to be.
2 A continuation of the vocational/liberal tension in conceptual discussions, with the emphasis moving back some way towards the liberal perspective at some point in the not too

distant future. This debate seems likely to be with us forever, but I do not yet detect much movement back towards the liberal perspective (too hopeful perhaps?).

3   A good deal of conceptual activity, stimulated by the growing policy debate, around the ideas of the learning organization and the learning society. This has definitely been a major area of conceptual activity during the last five years, though the learning organization may be being overtaken by the notion of knowledge management now. Similarly, the interest in the learning society has been paralleled by the resurgence of interest in the notion of lifelong education.

4   The development and popularization of additional concepts to do with further, higher, adult and continuing education and training; reflecting both the expansion and diversification of these areas of provision. This is evident in the increasing attention given to, for example, problem-based learning and modes of knowledge.

5   A growth in the area of work-related concepts, building upon the increasing prevalence of linkages between education and work. Definitely a major area of interest, as seen in the continuing attention paid to human capital and the rise of social capital as a concept.

6   The effective rejection of the idea of andragogy, and its replacement by other proto-theories to explain and understand adult education and training. I think we are still waiting for developments here.

7   Considerable activity around the concepts of competence and quality, to better define and critically assess their meanings and application. This has happened, at a detailed, practical level.

8   Further work on the ideas of success and failure, and outcomes, to more adequately recognize the multiple routes that are possible through and beyond education and training. There have been some developments here, but more is needed.

Overall, then, a fairly accurate set of predictions, though the details have differed from what I might have expected. My other specific prediction, or rather hope, was for the development of a new concept of 'learnership'. This concept was seen as referring to two aspects of adult education and training. First, it would recognize the active and continuing engagement of certain adults in learning, both over a considerable period of time and in a range of different settings. Second, it would reinforce these adults' recognition of this activity as an important, valid, related and integral engagement alongside other major life roles like worker, parent and partner. On this prediction, though I can detect some developments – e.g. in terms of policy, the government introduced the ill-fated notion of Individual Learning Accounts; while, in terms of analysis, there has been some exploration of the related idea of learning careers (Bloomer and Hodkinson 2000) – I think more are due.

Finally, do I have any new predictions? I do have one major one, and, in a sense, it is one that I missed last time. This is that the arena of adult education and training – and the concepts within it – will become more and more politicized. I think this will happen at two levels. Most obviously, at the national (and, of course, international) level, where adult education and training has become a major concern of government. But also, however, and more insidiously, at the institutional level, whether this be an educational institution or an employer in a more general sense. Here, the increased attention being paid to adult education and training will have a practical, and frequently compulsory, impact.

References

Advisory Council for Adult and Continuing Education (1982) *Continuing Education: from policies to practice*. Leicester, ACACE.

Allen, I (1994) *Doctors and Their Careers: a new generation*. London, Policy Studies Institute.

Allman, P (1983) 'The nature and process of adult development', pp. 107–23 in M Tight (ed.) *Adult Learning and Education*. London, Croom Helm.

Argyris, C (1992) *On Organizational Learning*. Oxford, Blackwell.

Argyris, C and Schön, D (1978) *Organizational Learning: a theory of action perspective*. Reading, MA, Addison-Wesley.

Arnold, J (1997) *Managing Careers into the 21st Century*. London, Paul Chapman.

Arthur, M, Inkson, K, and Pringle, J (1999) *The New Careers: individual action and economic change*. London, Sage.

Ashworth, A and Harvey, R (1994) *Assessing Quality in Further and Higher Education*. London, Jessica Kingsley.

Ashworth, P and Saxton, J (1990) 'On competence'. *Journal of Further and Higher Education*, 14, 2, pp. 3–25.

Askling, B, Henkel, M, and Kehm, B (2001) 'Concepts of knowledge and their organisation in universities'. *European Journal of Education*, 36, 3, pp. 341–50.

Aspin, D, and Chapman, J (2000) 'Lifelong learning: concepts and conceptions'. *International Journal of Lifelong Education*, 19, 1, pp. 2–19.

Avis, J (1991) 'Not so radical after all? Access, credit levels and the learner'. *Journal of Access Studies*, 6, 1, pp. 40–51.

Bagnall, R (1990) 'Lifelong education: the institutionalization of an illiberal and regressive concept?' *Educational Philosophy and Theory*, 22, 1, pp. 1–7.

Bagnall, R (2000) 'Lifelong learning and the limitations of economic determinism'. *International Journal of Lifelong Education*, 19, 1, pp. 20–35.

Bailey, C (1992) 'Enterprise and liberal education: some reservations'. *Journal of the Philosophy of Education*, 26, 1, pp. 99–106.

Banks, M, Bates, I, Breakwell, G, Bynner, J, Euler, N, Jamieson, L, and Roberts, K (1992) *Careers and Identities*. Buckingham, Open University Press.

Baptiste, I (2001) 'Educating lone wolves: pedagogical implications of human capital theory'. *Adult Education Quarterly*, 51, 3, pp. 184–201.

Barnett, R (1990) *The Idea of Higher Education*. Buckingham, Open University Press.

Barnett, R (1994) *The Limits of Competence: knowledge, higher education and society*. Buckingham, Open University Press.

Barnett, R (1997) *Higher Education: a critical business*. Buckingham, Open University Press.

Barnett, R, Parry, G, Cox, R, Loder, C and Williams, G (1994) *Assessment of the Quality of Higher Education: a review and an evaluation*. London, Institute of Education.

Baron, S, Field, J and Schuller, T (eds) (2000) *Social Capital: critical perspectives*. Oxford, Oxford University Press.

Barrow, R and Milburn, G (1990) *A Critical Dictionary of Educational Concepts: an appraisal of selected ideas and issues in educational theory and practice*. Hemel Hempstead, Harvester Wheatsheaf, second edition.

Barrow, R and White, P (eds) (1993) *Beyond Liberal Education: essays in honour of Paul Hirst*. London, Routledge.

Becher, T (1994) 'The state and the university curriculum in Britain'. *European Journal of Education*, 29, 3, pp. 231–45.

Becher, T (1999) *Professional Practices: commitment and capability in a changing environment*. New Brunswick, NJ, Transaction Publishers.

Beck, U (2000) *What is Globalization?* Cambridge, Polity.

Becker, G (1993) *Human Capital: a theoretical and empirical analysis with special reference to education*. Chicago, IL, University of Chicago Press, third edition.

Beinart, S and Smith, P (1997) *National Adult Learning Survey 1997*. London, Department for Education and Employment.

Bell, D (1973) *The Coming of Post-industrial Society: a venture in social forecasting*. New York, Basic Books.

Bell, R and Tight, M (1993) *Open Universities: a British tradition?* Buckingham, Open University Press.

Benner, P (1984) *From Novice to Expert: excellence and power in clinical nursing*. Menlo Park, CA, Addison-Wesley.

Bennett, R and McCoshan, A (1993) *Enterprise and Human Resource Development: local capacity building*. London, Paul Chapman.

Bines, H and Watson, D (1992) *Developing Professional Education*. Buckingham, Open University Press.

Blackledge, D and Hunt, B (1985) *Sociological Interpretations of Education*. London, Routledge.

Blaxter, L and Hughes, C (2000) 'Social capital: a critique', pp. 80–93 in J Thompson (ed.) *Stretching the Academy: the politics and practice of widening participation in higher education*. Leicester, National Institute of Adult Continuing Education.

Blaug, M (1992) *The Methodology of Economics: or how economists explain*. Cambridge, Cambridge University Press, second edition.

Bligh, D, Thomas, H and McNay, I (1999) *Understanding Higher Education: an introduction for parents, staff, employers and students*. Exeter, Intellect.

Bloomer, M and Hodkinson, P (2000) 'Learning careers: continuity and change in young people's dispositions to learning', *British Educational Research Journal*, 26, 5, pp. 583–97.

Boot, R and Hodgson, V (1987) 'Open learning: meaning and experience', pp. 5–15 in V Hodgson, S Mann and R Snell (eds) *Beyond Distance Teaching Towards Open Learning*. Milton Keynes, Open University Press.

Boshier, R *et al.* (1980) *Towards a Learning Society: New Zealand adult education in transition*. Auckland, Learning Press.

Bosworth, D (1991) *Open Learning*. London, Cassell.

Boud, D, Cohen, R and Walker, D (eds) (1993) *Using Experience for Learning*. Buckingham, Open University Press.

Boud, D, and Feletti (1997) 'Changing problem-based learning', pp. 1–14 in D Boud, and G Feletti (eds) *The Challenge of Problem-based Learning*. London, Kogan Page, second edition.

Boud, D and Higgs, J (1993) 'Bringing self-directed learning into the mainstream of tertiary education', pp. 158–73 in N Graves (ed.) *Learner Managed Learning: practice, theory and policy*. Leeds, Higher Education for Capability.

Boud, D, Keogh, R and Walker, D (1985) 'Promoting reflection in learning: a model', pp. 18–40 in D Boud, R Keogh and D Walker (eds) *Reflection: turning experience into learning*. London, Kogan Page.

Boud, D and Miller, N (eds.) (1996) *Working with Experience: animating learning*. London, Routledge.

Bourdieu, P (1997) 'The forms of capital', pp. 46–58 in A Halsey, H Lauder, P Brown and A Wells (eds) *Education: culture, economy and society*. Oxford, Oxford University Press.

Bourdieu, P and Passeron, J-C (1990) *Reproduction in Education, Society and Culture*. London, Sage, second edition, translated by R Nice.

Bourner, T, Reynolds, A, Hamed, M and Barnett, R (1991) *Part-time Students and Their Experience of Higher Education*. Buckingham, Open University Press.

Bowles, S and Gintis, H (1976) *Schooling in Capitalist America: educational reform and the contradictions of economic life*. London, Routledge.

Boydell, T (1976) *Experiential Learning*. Manchester, University of Manchester Department of Adult Education.

Boys, C and Kirkland, J (1988) *Degrees of Success: career aspirations and destinations of college, university and polytechnic graduates*. London, Jessica Kingsley.

Bradshaw, D (1992) 'Classifications and models of transferable skills', pp. 39–115 in H Eggins (ed.) *Arts Graduates, Their Skills and Their Employment*. London, Falmer Press.

Brady, L (1985) *Models and Methods of Teaching*. Sydney, Prentice-Hall.

Brandes, D, and Ginnis, P (1986) *A Guide to Student-centred Learning*. Hemel Hempstead, Simon & Schuster.

Brennan, J (1989) 'Access courses', pp. 51–63 in O Fulton (ed.) *Access and Institutional Change*. Milton Keynes, Open University Press.

Brennan, J, de Vries, P and Williams, R (eds) (1997) *Standards and Quality in Higher Education*. London, Jessica Kingsley.

Bridges, D (1993) 'Transferable skills: a philosophical perspective'. *Studies in Higher Education*, 18, 1, pp. 43–51.

Brookfield, S (1983) *Adult Learners, Adult Education and the Community*. Milton Keynes, Open University Press.

Brookfield, S (1984) 'Self-directed adult learning: a critical paradigm'. *Adult Education Quarterly*, 35, 2, pp. 59–71.

Brookfield, S (1986) *Understanding and Facilitating Adult Learning*. San Francisco, CA, Jossey-Bass.

Brookfield, S (2000) 'Self-directed learning as a political idea', pp. 9–22 in G Straka (ed.) *Conceptions of Self-directed Learning: theoretical and conceptual considerations*. Munster, Waxmann.

Brown, A and Webb, J (1990) 'The higher education route to the labour market for mature students'. *British Journal of Education and Work*, 4, 1, pp. 5–21.

Brown, J and Duguid, P (2000) *The Social Life of Information*. Boston, MA, Harvard Business School Press.

Brown, P and Lauder, H (2000) 'Human capital, social capital and collective intelligence', pp. 226–42 in S Baron, J Field and T Schuller (eds) *Social Capital: critical perspectives*. Oxford, Oxford University Press.

Brown S and Smith, B (ed.) (1996) *Resource-based Learning*. London, Kogan Page.

Buckley, R and Caple, J (1990) *The Theory and Practice of Training*. London, Kogan Page.

Burgess, T (ed.) (1986) *Education for Capability*. Windsor, NFER-Nelson.

Burgoyne, J, Pedler, M and Boydell, T (eds) (1994) *Towards the Learning Company: concepts and practices*. Maidenhead, McGraw-Hill.

Burke, J (1991) 'Competence and higher education: implications for institutions and professional bodies', pp. 22–46 in P Raggatt and L Unwin (eds) *Change and Intervention: vocational education and training*. London, Falmer Press.

Burke, J (ed.) (1995) *Outcomes, Learning and the Curriculum: implications for NVQs, GNVQs and other qualifications*. London, Falmer Press.

Burke, P (2002) *Accessing Education: effectively widening participation*. Stoke-on-Trent, Trentham Books.

Burnard, P (1988) 'Experiential learning: some theoretical considerations'. *International Journal of Lifelong Education*, 7, 2, pp. 127–33.

Burton, L (ed.) (1992) *Developing Resourceful Humans: adult education within the economic context*. London, Routledge.

Bynner, J (1992) 'The rise of open learning: a UK approach to work-related education and training', *International Journal of Lifelong Education*, 11, 2, pp. 103–14.

Cabrera, A, Castañeda, M, Nara, A and Hengstler, D (1992) 'The convergence between two theories of college persistence'. *Journal of Higher Education*, 63, 2, pp. 143–64.

Calder, J and McCollum, A (1998) *Open and Flexible Learning in Vocational Education and Training*. London, Kogan Page.

Campaign for Learning (1998) *Attitudes to Learning '98. MORI state of the nation survey: summary report*. London, Campaign for Learning.

Campanelli, P, Channell, J, McAulay, L, Renouf, A and Thomas, R (1994) *Training: an exploration of the word and the concept with an analysis of the implications for survey design*. Sheffield, Employment Department.

Candy, P, Harri-Augstein, S and Thomas, L (1985) 'Reflection and the self-organised learner: a model of learning conversations', pp. 100–16 in D Boud, R Keogh and D Walker (eds) *Reflection: turning experience into learning*. London, Kogan Page.

Cantor, L, Roberts, I and Pratley, B (1995) *A Guide to Further Education in England and Wales*. London, Cassell.

Cara, S, Landry, C and Ranson, S (1998) *The Learning City in the Learning Age*. London, Comedia and Demos.

Carmen, R (1995) 'Workshop for enterprise management versus "British" enterprise education: the difference is in the context'. *Convergence*, 28, 1, pp. 72–88.

Carnegie Commission on Higher Education (1973) *Towards a Learning Society: alternative channels to life, work and service*. New York, McGraw-Hill.

Carnevale, A (1992) 'Human capital: a high-yield investment', pp. 48–71 in L Burton (ed.) *Developing Resourceful Humans: adult education within the economic context*. London, Routledge.

Carré, P (2000) 'From intentional to self-directed learning', pp. 49–57 in G Straka (ed.) *Conceptions of Self-directed Learning: theoretical and conceptual considerations*. Munster, Waxmann.

Castells, M (1996) *The Rise of the Network Society*. Oxford, Blackwell.

Challis, M (1993) *Introducing APEL*. London, Routledge.

Chapman, P (1993) *The Economics of Training*. London, Harvester Wheatsheaf.

Clark, D (1987) 'The concept of community education', pp. 50–69 in G Allen, J Bastiani, I Martin and K Richards (eds) *Community Education: an agenda for educational reform*. Milton Keynes, Open University Press.

Clyne, S (ed.) (1995) *Continuing Professional Development: perspectives on CPD in practice*. London, Kogan Page.

Coffield, F (1990) 'From the decade of enterprise culture to the decade of TECs'. *British Journal of Education and Work*, 4, 1, pp. 59–78.

Coffield, F (1998) 'A tale of three little pigs: building the learning society with straw'. *Evaluation and Research in Education*, 12, 1, pp. 44–58.

Coffield, F (1999) 'Breaking the consensus: lifelong learning as social control'. *British Educational Research Journal*, 25, 4, pp. 479–99.

Coleman, J (1990) *Foundations of Social Theory*. Cambridge, MA, Harvard University Press.

Collis, B and Moonen, J (2001) *Flexible Learning in a Digital World: experiences and expectations*. London, Kogan Page.

Commission on Post-secondary Education in Ontario (1972) *The Learning Society*. Toronto, Ministry of Government Services.

Cookson, P (1986) 'A framework for theory and research on adult education participation'. *Adult Education Quarterly*, 36, 3, pp. 130–41.

Coombs, P (1968) *The World Educational Crisis: a systems analysis*. Oxford, Oxford University Press.

Coombs, P (1985) *The World Crisis in Education: the view from the eighties.* Oxford, Oxford University Press.

Coombs, P and Ahmed, M (1974) *Attacking Rural Poverty: how nonformal education can help.* Baltimore, MD, Johns Hopkins University Press.

Coopey, J (1996) 'Crucial gaps in "the learning organization": power, politics and ideology', pp. 348–67 in K Starkey (ed.) *How Organizations Learn.* London, International Thomson Business Press.

Corlett, J (1998) 'Supporting the university for industry: the lessons of the Open College'. *Open Learning*, 13, 1, pp. 51–7.

Courtney, S (1992) *Why Adults Learn: towards a theory of participation in adult education.* London, Routledge.

Craft, A (ed.) (1994) *Quality Assurance in Higher Education: proceedings of an international conference.* London, Falmer Press.

Critten, P (1993) *Investing in People: towards corporate capability.* London, Butterworth Heinemann.

Crombie, A and Harries-Jenkins, G (1983) *The Demise of the Liberal Tradition: two essays on the future of British university adult education.* Leeds, University of Leeds, Department of Adult and Continuing Education.

Cropley, A (1979) 'Introduction', pp. 1–7 in A Cropley (ed.) *Lifelong Education: a stocktaking.* Hamburg, UNESCO Institute for Education.

Cross, K (1981) *Adults as Learners: increasing participation and facilitating learning.* San Francisco, CA, Jossey-Bass.

Cummings, W (1995) 'The Asian human resource approach in global perspective'. *Oxford Review of Education*, 21, 1, pp. 67–81.

Curran, C (2001) 'The phenomenon of on-line learning', *European Journal of Education*, 36, 2, pp. 113–32.

Curzon, L (1997) *Teaching in Further Education: an outline of principles and practice.* London, Cassell, fifth edition.

Cytrynbaum, S and Crites, J (1989) 'The utility of adult developmental theory in understanding career adjustment process', pp. 66–88 in M Arthur, D Hall, and B Lawrence (eds) *Handbook of Career Theory.* Cambridge, Cambridge University Press.

Darmon, I, Hadjivassiliou, K, Sommerlad, E, Stern, E, Turbin, J and Danau, D (1998) 'Continuing vocational training: key issues', pp. 23–36 in F Coffield (ed.) *Learning at Work.* Bristol, The Policy Press.

Davenport, J (1987) 'Is there any way out of the andragogy morass?' *Lifelong Learning: an omnibus of practice and research*, 2, 3, pp. 17–20.

Davies, P (ed.) (1995) *Adults in Higher Education: international experiences in access and participation.* London, Jessica Kingsley.

Dearden, R (1984) 'Education and training'. *Westminster Studies in Education*, 7, pp. 57–66.

Department of Education and Science (1980) *Continuing Education: post-experience vocational provision for those in employment.* London, DES.

Department of Employment (1991) *Flexible Learning: a framework for education and training in the skills decade.* Sheffield, Department of Employment.

Dixon, N (1994) *The Organizational Learning Cycle: how we can learn collectively.* Maidenhead, McGraw-Hill.

Doherty, G (ed.) (1994a) *Developing Quality Systems in Education*. London, Routledge.

Doherty, G (1994b) 'The concern for quality', pp. 3–34 in G Doherty (ed.) *Developing Quality Systems in Education*. London, Routledge.

Dolowitz, D, Hulme, R, Nellis, M and O'Neill, F (2000) *Policy Transfer and British Social Policy: learning from the USA?* Buckingham, Open University Press.

Dore, R (1976) *The Diploma Disease*. London, Allen and Unwin.

Dreyfus, H, Dreyfus, S and Athanasiou, T (1986) *Mind Over Machine: the power of human intuition and expertise in the era of the computer*. Oxford, Blackwell.

Drucker, P (1995) *Managing in a Time of Great Change*. Oxford, Butterworth-Heinemann.

Ecclestone, K (1994) 'Democratic values and purposes: the overlooked challenge of competence'. *Educational Studies*, 20, 2, pp. 155–66.

Economic and Social Research Council (1994) *Research Specification for the ESRC 'Learning Society: Knowledge and Skills for Employment' Programme*. Swindon, ESRC.

Edwards, J (1991) *Evaluation in Adult and Further Education: a practical handbook for teachers and organisers*. Liverpool, Workers' Educational Association.

Edwards, R (1995) 'Behind the banner: whither the learning society?' *Adults Learning*, 6, 6, pp. 187–9.

Edwards, R (1997) *Changing Places? Flexibility, lifelong learning and a learning society*. London, Routledge.

Edwards, R, Armstrong, P and Miller, N (2001) 'Include me out: critical readings of social exclusion, social inclusion and lifelong learning'. *International Journal of Lifelong Education*, 20, 5, pp. 417–28.

Elliott, G (1999) *Lifelong Learning: the politics of the new learning environment*. London, Jessica Kingsley.

Eraut, M (1990) 'Identifying the knowledge which underpins performance', pp. 22–8 in H Black and A Wolf (eds) *Knowledge and Competence: current issues in training and education*. Sheffield, Employment Department.

Eraut, M (1994) *Developing Professional Knowledge and Competence*. London, Falmer Press.

Eraut, M (1997) 'Perspectives on defining "The Learning Society"'. *Journal of Education Policy*, 12, 6, pp. 551–8.

Evans, B (1987) *Radical Adult Education: a political critique*. London, Croom Helm.

Evans, N (1992) *Experiential Learning: assessment and accreditation*. London, Routledge.

Evans, N (1994) *Experiential Learning for All*. London, Routledge.

Evans, N (ed.) (2000) *Experiential Learning Around the World: employability and the global economy*. London, Jessica Kingsley.

Evans, T and Nation, D (1992) 'Theorising open and distance learning'. *Open Learning*, 7, 2, pp. 3–13.

Evetts, J (ed.) (1994) *Women and Career: themes and issues in advanced industrialised societies*. Harlow, Longman.

Evetts, J (1996) *Gender and Career in Science and Engineering*. London, Taylor and Francis.

Fairbairn, A (1971) *The Leicestershire Community Colleges*. Leicester, National Institute of Adult Education.

Felstead, A and Jewson, N (eds) (1999) *Global Trends in Flexible Labour*. Basingstoke, Macmillan.

Fevre, R, Rees, G and Gorard, S (1999) 'Some sociological alternatives to human capital theory and their implications for research on post-compulsory education and training'. *Journal of Education and Work*, 12, 2, pp. 117–40.

Field, J (2001) 'Lifelong education'. *International Journal of Lifelong Education*, 20, 1–2, pp. 3–15.

Field, J, Schuller, T and Baron, S (2000) 'Social capital and human capital revisited', pp. 243–63 in S Baron, J Field and T Schuller (eds.) *Social Capital: critical perspectives*. Oxford, Oxford University Press.

Field, M (1993) *APL: developing more flexible colleges*. London, Routledge.

Fletcher, C (1989) 'Community education and community development', pp. 51–54 in C Titmus (ed.) *Lifelong Education for Adults: an international handbook*. Oxford, Pergamon.

Fletcher, S (1991) *NVQs, Standards and Competence: a practical guide for employers, managers and trainers*. London, Kogan Page.

Flew, A (ed.) (1956) *Essays in Conceptual Analysis*. London, Macmillan.

Fordham, P (ed.) (1980) *Participation, Learning and Change: Commonwealth approaches to non-formal education*. London, Commonwealth Secretariat.

Fordham, P, Poulton, G and Randle, L (1979) *Learning Networks in Adult Education: non-formal education on a housing estate*. London, Routledge and Kegan Paul.

Foreman-Peck, L (1993) 'Enterprise education: a new social ethic for higher education'. *Vocational Aspect of Education*, 45, 2, pp. 99–111.

Forrester, K, Payne, J and Ward, K (1995) *Workplace Learning: perspectives on education, training and work*. Aldershot, Avebury.

Foster, P (1987) 'The contribution of education to development', pp. 93–100 in G Psacharopoulos (ed.) *Economics of Education: research and studies*. Oxford, Pergamon.

Francis, B and Penn, R (1994) 'Towards a phenomenology of skill', pp. 223–43 in R Penn, M Rose and J Rubery (eds) *Skill and Occupational Change*. Oxford, Oxford University Press.

Freedman, L (1987) *Quality in Continuing Education: principles, practices and standards for colleges and universities*. San Francisco, CA, Jossey-Bass.

Freire, P (1972) *Pedagogy of the Oppressed*. Translated by M Ramer. Harmondsworth, Penguin.

Freire, P (1974) *Education for Critical Consciousness*. London, Sheed and Ward.

Further Education Unit (1983) *Flexible Learning Opportunities*. London, Further Education Unit.

Further Education Unit (1984) *Flexible Learning in Action*. London, Further Education Unit.

Gagné, R (1985) *The Conditions of Learning and Theory of Instruction.* New York, Holt, Rinehart and Winston, fourth edition.

Gallie, D and White, M (1993) *Employee Commitment and the Skills Revolution.* London, Policy Studies Institute.

Garavan, T (1997a) 'The learning organization: a review and evaluation'. *The Learning Organization,* 4, 1, pp. 18–29.

Garavan, T (1997b) 'Training, development, education and learning: different or the same?' *Journal of European Industrial Training,* 21, 2, pp. 39–50.

Garavan, T, Heraty, N and Barnicle, B (1999) 'Human resource development literature: current issues, priorities and dilemmas'. *Journal of European Industrial Training,* 23, 4/5, pp. 169–79.

Garrick, J (1998) *Informal Learning in the Workplace: unmasking human resource development.* London, Routledge.

Garrison, D (1989) *Understanding Distance Education: a framework for the future.* London, Routledge.

Garrison, D and Shale, D (1990) 'Tilting at windmills? Destroying mythology in distance education'. *International Council for Distance Education Bulletin,* 24, pp. 42–6.

Gibbons, M, Limoges, C, Nowotny, H, Schwartzman, S, Scott, P and Trow, M (1994) *The New Production of Knowledge: the dynamics of science and research in contemporary societies.* London, Sage.

Gibson, A (1994) 'Freirean versus enterprise education: the difference is in the business'. *Convergence,* 27, 1, pp. 46–57.

Glaser, R and Chi, M (1988) 'Overview', pp. xv–xxviii in M Chi, R Glaser and M Farr (eds) *The Nature of Expertise.* Hillsdale, NJ, Laurence Erlbaum Associates.

Glatter, R, Wedell, E, Harris, W and Subramanian, S (1971) *Study by Correspondence: an enquiry into correspondence study for examinations for degrees and other advanced qualifications.* London, Longman.

Goldschmidt, W (1990) *The Human Career: the self in the symbolic world.* Oxford, Blackwell.

Goldstein, I and Gessner, M (1988) 'Training and development in work organisations'. *International Review of Industrial and Organisational Psychology,* pp. 43–72.

Goodson, I and Hargreaves, A (eds) (1996) *Teachers' Professional Lives.* London, Falmer Press.

Graves, N (ed.) (1993) *Learner Managed Learning: practice, theory and policy.* Leeds, Higher Education for Capability.

Gray, J (2000) 'Inclusion: a radical critique', pp. 19–36 in P Askonas and A Stewart (eds), *Social Inclusion: possibilities and tensions.* Basingstoke, Macmillan.

Green, D (1994) 'What is quality in higher education? Concepts, policy and practice', pp. 3–20 in D Green (ed.) *What is Quality in Higher Education?* Buckingham, Open University Press.

Griffin, C (1983) *Curriculum Theory in Adult and Lifelong Education.* London, Croom Helm.

Griffin, C and Brownhill, B (2001) 'The learning society', pp. 55–68 in P Jarvis (ed.) *The Age of Learning: education and the knowledge society.* London, Kogan Page.

Groombridge, B (1983) 'Adult education and the education of adults', pp. 3–19 in M Tight (ed.) *Adult Learning and Education*. London, Croom Helm.

Grundy, T (1994) *Strategic Learning in Action: how to accelerate and sustain business change*. Maidenhead, McGraw-Hill.

Halford, S, Savage, M and Witz, A (1997) *Gender, Careers and Organisations: current developments in banking, nursing and local government*. Basingstoke, Macmillan.

Halsey, A (1992) 'An international comparison of access to higher education'. *Oxford Studies in Comparative Education*, 1, 1, pp. 11–36.

Halsey, A (1993) 'Trends in access and equity in higher education: Britain in international perspective'. *Oxford Review of Education*, 19, 2, pp. 129–40.

Hamilton, E (1992) *Adult Education for Community Development*. Westport, CT, Greenwood Press.

Harris, D (1987) *Openness and Closure in Distance Education*. London, Falmer Press.

Harris, D and Bell, C (1990) *Evaluating and Assessing for Learning*. London, Kogan Page, second edition.

Harrison, R (1992) *Employee Development*. London, Institute of Personnel Management.

Harrison, R (2000) *Employee Development*. London, Chartered Institute of Personnel and Development, second edition.

Harry, K (ed.) (1999) *Higher Education Through Open and Distance Learning*. London, Routledge.

Hayes, C, Fonda, N and Hillman, J (1995) *Learning in the New Millennium*. London, National Commission on Education.

Hendry, C (1996) 'Understanding and creating whole organizational change through learning theory'. *Human Relations*, 49, 5, pp. 621–41.

Her Majesty's Inspectors (1992) *A Survey of the Enterprise in Higher Education Initiative in Fifteen Polytechnics and Colleges of Higher Education, September 1989–March 1991*. London, Department of Education and Science.

Heron, J (1989) *The Facilitators' Handbook*. London, Kogan Page.

Hettne, B (1990) *Development Theory and the Three Worlds*. Harlow, Longman.

Hewitt, P (1993) *About Time: the revolution in work and family life*. London, Institute for Public Policy Research.

Higher Education Quality Council (1994) *Choosing to Change: extending access, choice and mobility in higher education*. London, HEQC.

Higher Education Quality Council (1996) *Modular Higher Education in the UK: in focus*. London, HEQC.

Hill, V (1994) *Further Education in the United Kingdom*. London, Collins Educational/Further Education Staff College, second edition.

Hirschham, L, Gilmore, T and Newell, T (1989) 'Training and learning in a post-industrial World', pp. 185–200 in H Leymann and H Kornbluh (eds) *Socialization and Learning at Work: a new approach to the learning process in the workplace and society*. Aldershot, Avebury.

Hirst, P (1974) *Knowledge and the Curriculum: a collection of philosophical papers*. London, Routledge and Kegan Paul.

Hirst, P and Peters, R (1970) *The Logic of Education*. London, Routledge.
Hobart, M (ed.) (1993) *An Anthropological Critique of Development: the growth of ignorance*. London, Routledge.
Hobsbawm, E and Ranger, T (eds.) (1983) *The Invention of Tradition*. Cambridge, Cambridge University Press.
Hodkinson, P and Issitt, M (eds) (1995) *The Challenge of Competence: professionalism through vocational education and training*. London, Cassell.
Holford, J, Jarvis, P and Griffin, C (eds) (1998) *International Perspectives on Lifelong Learning*. London, Kogan Page.
Holmberg, B (1986) *Growth and Structure of Distance Education*. Beckenham, Croom Helm.
Holmberg, B (1997) 'Distance-education theory again'. *Open Learning*, 12, 1, pp. 31–9.
Houle, C (1974) *The External Degree*. San Francisco, CA, Jossey-Bass.
Hoyle, E and John, P (1995) *Professional Knowledge and Professional Practice*. London, Cassell.
Hudson, R, Maslin-Prothero, S and Oates, L (eds) (1997) *Flexible Learning in Action: case studies in higher education*. London, Kogan Page.
Hughes, C (1999) 'The dire in self-directed learning'. *Adults Learning*, 11, 2, pp. 7–9.
Hughes, C (2002) *Women's Contemporary Lives: within and beyond the mirror*. London, Routledge.
Hughes, C and Tight, M (1995) 'The myth of the learning society'. *British Journal of Educational Studies*, 43, 3, pp. 290–304.
Husen, T (1974) *The Learning Society*. London, Methuen.
Husen, T (1986) *The Learning Society Revisited*. Oxford, Pergamon.
Hyland, T (1994) *Competence, Education and NVQs: dissenting perspectives*. London, Cassell.
Illich, I (1973) *Deschooling Society*. Harmondsworth, Penguin.
Jallade, J-P and Mora, J-G (2001) 'Lifelong learning: international injunctions and university practices'. *European Journal of Education*, 36, 3, pp. 361–77.
Jarvis, P (1987) *Adult Learning in the Social Context*. London, Croom Helm.
Jarvis, P (1990) *An International Dictionary of Adult and Continuing Education*. London, Routledge.
Jarvis, P (1995) *Adult and Continuing Education: theory and practice*. London, Routledge, second edition.
Jarvis, P (1998) 'Paradoxes of the learning society', pp. 59–68 in J Holford, P Jarvis and C Griffin (eds) *International Perspectives on Lifelong Learning*. London, Kogan Page.
Jarvis, P (2001a) 'Malcolm S Knowles', pp. 144–59 in P Jarvis (ed.) *Twentieth Century Thinkers in Adult and Continuing Education*. London, Kogan Page, second edition.
Jarvis, P (2001b) *Universities and Corporate Universities: the higher learning industry in global society*. London, Kogan Page.
Jenson, D, Gray, J and Sime, N (1991) *Participation, Progress and Performance in Post-compulsory Education*. Sheffield, Employment Department.

Jessup, G (1989) 'The emerging model of vocational education and training', pp. 65–76 in J Burke (ed.) *Competency Based Education and Training*. London, Falmer Press.

Jessup, G (1991) *Outcomes: NVQs and the Emerging Model of Education and Training*. London, Falmer Press.

Johnes, G (1993) *The Economics of Education*. London, Macmillan.

Johnston, R (1997) 'Distance learning: medium or massage?' *Journal of Further and Higher Education*, 21, 1, pp. 107–22.

Johnston, R (2000) 'Community education and lifelong learning: local spice for global fare?', pp. 12–28 in J Field and M Leicester (eds) *Lifelong Learning: education across the lifespan*. London, RoutledgeFalmer.

Jones, A (1995) 'A learning in organizations model', pp. 111–30 in D Bradshaw (ed.) *Bringing Learning to Life: the learning revolution, the economy and the individual*. London, Falmer.

Jones, A and Hendry, C (1992) *The Learning Organization: a review of literature and practice*. London, HRD Partnership.

Jones, A and Hendry, C (1994) 'The learning organisation: adult learning and organisational transformation'. *British Journal of Management*, 5, pp. 153–62.

Jones, S and Joss, R (1995) 'Models of professionalism', pp. 15–33 in M Yelloly and M Henkel (eds) *Learning and Teaching in Social Work: towards reflective practice*. London, Jessica Kingsley.

Joyce, B, Calhoun, E and Hopkins, D (1997) *Models of Learning: tools for teaching*. Buckingham, Open University Press.

Joyce, B, Weil, M and Showers, B (1992) *Models of Teaching*. Boston, MA, Allyn and Bacon, fourth edition.

Kanter, R (1989) *When Giants Learn to Dance: mastering the challenges of strategy, management and career in the 1990s*. New York, Simon and Schuster.

Kaye, A and Rumble, G (1991) 'Open universities: a comparative approach', *Prospects*, 21, 2, pp. 214–26.

Keegan, D (1986) *The Foundations of Distance Education*. Beckenham, Croom Helm.

Keegan, D (1989) 'Problems in defining the field of distance education', pp. 8–15 in M Moore and G Clark (eds) *Readings in Principles of Distance Education*. American Center for the Study of Distance Education, College Station, PA, Pennsylvania State University.

Keegan, D (ed.) (1994) *Otto Peters on Distance Education: the industrialization of teaching and learning*. London, Routledge.

Keep, E, and Rainbird, H (2000) 'Towards the learning organization?', pp. 173–94 in S Bach, and K Sisson (eds) *Personnel Management in Britain*. Oxford, Blackwell, third edition.

Kelly, A (1999) *The Curriculum: theory and practice*. London, Paul Chapman, fourth edition.

Kennedy, H (1997) *Learning Works: widening participation in further education*. Coventry, Further Education Funding Council.

Kerckhoff, A (1993) *Diverging Pathways: social structure and career deflections*. Cambridge, Cambridge University Press.

Kidd, J and Titmus, C (1989) 'Introduction', pp. xxiii–xxxix in C Titmus (ed.) *Lifelong Education for Adults: an international handbook*. Oxford, Pergamon.

Kim, D (1993) 'The link between individual and organizational learning'. *Sloan Management Review*, 35, 1, pp. 37–50.

Kirkwood, G and Kirkwood, C (1989) *Living Adult Education: Freire in Scotland*. Edinburgh, Scottish Institute of Adult and Continuing Education/Open University Press.

Knapper, C and Cropley, A (2000) *Lifelong Learning in Higher Education*. London, Kogan Page, third edition.

Knowles, M (1970) *The Modern Practice of Adult Education: from pedagogy to andragogy*. Cambridge Book Company.

Knowles, M (1973) *The Adult Learner: a neglected species*. Houston, TX, Gulf Publishing Co.

Knowles, M (1985) *Andragogy in Action: applying modern principles of adult learning*. San Francisco, CA, Jossey-Bass.

Kogan, M (2000) 'Lifelong learning in the UK', *European Journal of Education*, 35, 3, pp. 341–59.

Kolb, D (1984) *Experiential Learning: experience as the source of learning and development*. Englewood Cliffs, NJ, Prentice Hall.

Kolb, D, Lublin, S, Spoth, J and Baker, R (1986) 'Strategic management development: using experiential learning to assess and develop managerial competences'. *Journal of Management Development*, 5, 3, pp. 13–24.

Krajnc, A (1989) 'Andragogy', pp. 19–21 in C Titmus (ed.) *Lifelong Education for Adults: an international handbook*. Oxford, Pergamon.

Lave, J and Wenger, E (1991) *Situated Learning: legitimate peripheral participation*. Cambridge, Cambridge University Press.

Lawson, K (1982) 'Lifelong education: concept or policy?' *International Journal of Lifelong Education*, 1, 2, pp. 97–108.

Lawton, D and Gordon, P (1993) *Dictionary of Education*. London, Routledge.

Layard, R, Mayhew, K and Owen, G (eds) (1994) *Britain's Training Deficit*. Aldershot, Avebury.

Lea, M and Nicoll, K (eds) (2002) *Distributed Learning: social and cultural approaches to practice*. London, RoutledgeFalmer.

Lengrand, P (1989) 'Lifelong education: growth of the concept', pp. 5–9 in C Titmus (ed.) *Lifelong Education for Adults: an international handbook*. Oxford, Pergamon.

Lessem, R (1993) *Business as a Learning Community: applying global concepts to organizational learning*. Maidenhead, McGraw-Hill.

Levitas, R (1998) *The Inclusive Society? Social exclusion and new labour*. Basingstoke, Macmillan.

Lewis, R (1986) 'What is open learning?' *Open Learning*, 1 (2), pp. 5–10.

Lewis, R and Spencer, D (1986) *What is Open Learning?* London, Council for Educational Technology.

Lister, R (2000) 'Strategies for social inclusion: promoting social cohesion or social justice?', pp. 37–54 in P Askonas and A Stewart (eds), *Social Inclusion: possibilities and tensions*. Basingstoke, Macmillan.

Lloyd, C and Cook, A (1993) *Implementing Standards of Competence: practical strategies for industry*. London, Kogan Page.

Lockwood, F (2001) 'Innovation in distributed learning: creating the environment', pp. 1–14 in F Lockwood and A Gooley (eds) *Innovation in Open and Distance Learning: successful development of online and web-based learning*. London, Kogan Page.

Long, D (1990) *Learner Managed Learning: the key to lifelong learning and development*. London, Kogan Page.

Lovett, T (1982) *Adult Education, Community Development and the Working Class*. Nottingham, University of Nottingham Department of Adult Education, second edition.

Lovett, T, Clarke, C and Kilmurray, A (1983) *Adult Education and Community Action*. London, Croom Helm.

Lum, G (1999) 'Where's the competence in competence-based education and training?' *Journal of Philosophy of Education*, 33, 3, pp. 403–18.

Mabey, C and Iles, P (1994) 'Career development·practices in the UK: a participant perspective', pp. 123–32 in C Mabey and P Iles (eds), *Managing Learning*. London, Routledge.

MacDonald, R and Coffield, F (1991) *Risky Business? Youth and the enterprise culture*. London, Falmer Press.

MacKenzie, N, Postgate, R and Scupham, J (1975) *Open Learning: systems and problems in post-secondary education*. Paris, UNESCO.

Mackie, R (ed.) (1980) *Literacy and Revolution: the pedagogy of Paulo Freire*. London, Pluto Press.

Maguire, M, Maguire, S and Felstead, A (1993) *Factors Influencing Individual Commitment to Lifetime Learning: a literature review*. Sheffield, Employment Department.

Margetson, D (1997) 'Why is problem-based learning a challenge?', pp. 36–44 in D Boud and G Feletti (eds) *The Challenge of Problem-based Learning*. London, Kogan Page, second edition.

Marginson, S (1995) 'Markets in higher education: Australia', pp. 17–39 in J Smyth (ed.) *Academic Work*. Buckingham, Open University Press.

Marquardt, M and Reynolds, A (1994) *The Global Learning Organisation*. Burr Ridge, IL, Irwin Professional Publishing.

Marshall, J (1995) *Women Managers Moving On: exploring career and life choices*. London, Routledge.

Martin, I (1987) 'Community education: towards a theoretical analysis', pp. 9–32 in G Allen, J Bastiani, I Martin and K Richards (eds) *Community Education: an agenda for educational reform*. Milton Keynes, Open University Press.

Marton, F, Dall'Alba, G and Beaty, E (1993) 'Conceptions of learning'. *International Journal of Educational Research*, 19, 3, pp. 277–300.

Mason, R and Kaye, A (eds) (1989) *Mindweave: Communications, Computers and Distance Education*. Oxford, Pergamon Press.

Matthews, M (1980) 'Knowledge, action and power', pp. 82–92 in R Mackie (ed.) *Literacy and Revolution: the pedagogy of Paulo Freire*. London, Pluto Press.

Mayo, A and Lank, E (1994) *The Power of Learning: a guide to gaining competitive advantage*. London, Institute of Personnel and Development.

Mayo, M (1997) *Imagining Tomorrow: adult education for transformation.* Leicester, National Institute of Adult Continuing Education.

Mayo, P (1999) *Gramsci, Freire and Adult Education: possibilities for transformative action.* London, Zed Books.

McClenaghan, P (2000) 'Social capital: exploring the theoretical foundations of community development education', *British Educational Research Journal*, 26, 5, pp. 565–82.

McConnell, C (1982) 'Definitions, methods, paradigms', pp. 1–11 in L Bidwell and C McConnell (eds) *Community Education and Community Development.* Aberdeen, Northern College of Education.

McGill, I and Beaty, L (1992) *Action Learning: a practitioner's guide.* London, Kogan Page.

McGivney, V (1990) *Education's For Other People: access to education for non-participant adults.* Leicester, National Institute of Adult Continuing Education.

McGivney, V (1992) *Tracking Adult Learning Routes: a pilot investigation into adult learners' starting points and progression to further education and training.* Leicester, National Institute of Adult Continuing Education.

McGivney, V (1993) *Women, Education and Training: barriers to access, informal starting points and progression routes.* Leicester, National Institute of Adult Continuing Education.

McGivney, V (1996) *Staying or Leaving the Course: non-completion and retention of mature students in further and higher education.* Leicester, National Institute of Adult Continuing Education.

McIlroy, J and Spencer, B (1988) *University Adult Education in Crisis.* Leeds, University of Leeds, Department of Adult and Continuing Education.

McKenzie, P (1995) 'Education and training: still distinguishable?' *The Vocational Aspect of Education*, 47, 1, pp. 35–49.

McLaren, P and Lankshear, C (eds) (1994) *Politics of Liberation: paths from Freire.* London, Routledge.

McLean, G and McLean, L (2001) 'If we can't define HRD in one country, how can we define it in an international context?' *Human Resource Development International*, 4, 3, pp. 313–26.

McNay, I (1988) 'Open learning: a jarring note', pp. 130–9 in N Paine (ed.) *Open Learning in Transition: an agenda for action.* Cambridge, National Extension College.

Megginson, D, Joy-Matthews, J and Banfield, P (1993) *Human Resource Development.* London, Kogan Page.

Messick, S (ed) (1999) *Assessment in Higher Education: issues of access, quality, student development and public policy.* Mahwah, NJ, Lawrence Erlbaum.

Metcalf, H (1993) *Non-Traditional Students' Experience of Higher Education: a review of the literature.* London, Committee of Vice-Chancellors and Principals.

Mezirow, J (1981) 'A critical theory of adult learning and education'. *Adult Education Journal* (USA), 32, 1, pp. 3–24.

Miettinen, R (2000) 'The concept of experiential learning and John Dewey's theory of reflective thought and action'. *International Journal of Lifelong Education*, 19, 1, pp. 54–72.

Molloy, S and Carroll, V (1992) *Progress and Performance in Higher Education: a report on performance monitoring of 'standard' and 'non-standard' entrants to undergraduate courses*. London, Council for National Academic Awards.

Moore, M (1990) 'Recent contributions to the theory of distance education'. *Open Learning*, 5, 3, pp. 10–15.

Morgan, C and Murgatroyd, S (1994) *Total Quality Management in the Public Sector: an international perspective*. Buckingham, Open University Press.

Morris, H (2000) 'The origins, forms and effects of modularisation and semesterisation in ten UK-based business schools'. *Higher Education Quarterly*, 54, 3, pp. 239–58.

Nadler, L and Nadler, Z (eds) (1990) *The Handbook of Human Resource Development*. New York, John Wiley, second edition.

National Commission on Education (1993) *Learning to Succeed: a radical look at education today and a strategy for the future*. London, Heinemann.

Newell, H (2000) 'Managing careers', pp. 218–38 in S Bach and K Sisson (eds) *Personnel Management in Britain*. Oxford, Blackwell, third edition.

Newman, M (1979) *The Poor Cousin: a study of adult education*. London, George Allen and Unwin.

Nicholson, M and West, M (1988) *Managerial Job Change: men and women in transition*. Cambridge, Cambridge University Press.

Nicoll, K (1997) ' "Flexible learning" – unsettling practices'. *Studies in Continuing Education*, 19, 2, pp. 100–111.

Nowotny, H, Scott, P and Gibbons, M (2001) *Re-thinking Science: knowledge and the public in an age of uncertainty*. Cambridge, Polity Press.

Nyberg, D (ed.) (1975) *The Philosophy of Open Education*. London, Routledge and Kegan Paul.

Oakeshott, M (1967) 'Learning and teaching', pp. 156–76 in R Peters (ed.) *The Concept of Education*. London, Routledge and Kegan Paul.

Organisation for Economic Cooperation and Development (1977) *Learning Opportunities for Adults. Volume IV: Participation in Adult Education*. Paris, OECD.

Palomba, C and Banta, T (1999) *Assessment Essentials: planning, implementing and improving assessment in higher education*. San Francisco, CA, Jossey-Bass.

Parry, G and Wake, C (1990) (eds) *Access and Alternative Futures for Higher Education*. London, Hodder and Stoughton.

Pascarella, E and Terenzini, P (1991) *How College Affects Students: findings and insights from twenty years of research*. San Francisco, CA, Jossey-Bass.

Paterson, R (1979) *Values, Education and the Adult*. London, Routledge and Kegan Paul.

Paul, R (1990) *Open Learning and Open Management: leadership and integrity in distance education*. London, Kogan Page.

Pedler, M, Burgoyne, J and Boydell, T (1991) *The Learning Company: a strategy for sustainable development*. London, McGraw-Hill.

Peelo, M and Wareham, T (2002) *Failing Students in Higher Education*. Buckingham, Open University Press.

Percy-Smith, J (2000) 'Introduction: the contours of social exclusion', pp. 1–21 in J Percy-Smith (ed.) *Policy Responses to Social Exclusion: towards inclusion?* Buckingham, Open University Press.

Perraton, H (1987) 'Theories, generalisation and practice in distance education'. *Open Learning*, 2 (3), pp. 3–12.

Perraton, J (2000) 'The consequences of globalization and corporate structures for projects of social inclusion', pp. 123–39 in P Askonas and A Stewart (eds), *Social Inclusion: possibilities and tensions.* Basingstoke, Macmillan.

Perry, W (1976) *Open University: a personal account by the first vice-chancellor.* Milton Keynes, Open University Press.

Peters, O (1983) 'Distance education and industrial production: a comparative interpretation in outline', pp. 95–113 in D Sewart, D Keegan and B Holmberg (eds) *Distance Education: international perspectives.* Beckenham, Croom Helm.

Peters, R (1966) *Ethics and Education.* London, George Allen and Unwin.

Peters, R (ed.) (1967) *The Concept of Education.* London, Routledge and Kegan Paul.

Peters, T (1987) *Thriving on Chaos.* London, Macmillan.

Phillips, A and Taylor, B (1986) 'Sex and skill', pp. 54–66 in Feminist Review (ed.) *Waged Work: a reader.* London, Virago.

Pineau, G (2000) 'Self-directed learning in the life course', pp. 127–41 in G Straka (ed.) *Conceptions of Self-directed Learning: theoretical and conceptual considerations.* Munster, Waxmann.

Plant, R (1974) *Community and Ideology: an essay in applied social philosophy.* London, Routledge and Kegan Paul.

Pollert, A (ed.) (1991) *Farewell to Flexibility?* Oxford, Blackwell.

Poster, C and Kruger, A (eds) (1990) *Community Education in the Western World.* London, Routledge.

Poster, C and Zimmer, J (eds) (1992) *Community Education in the Third World.* London, Routledge.

Preston, P (1996) *Development Theory: an introduction.* Oxford, Blackwell.

Pring, R (1993) 'Liberal education and vocational preparation', pp. 49–78 in R Barrow and P White (eds) *Beyond Liberal Education: essays in honour of Paul Hirst.* London, Routledge.

Prosser, M, Trigwell, K and Taylor, P (1994) 'A phenomenographic study of academics' conceptions of science learning and teaching'. *Learning and Instruction*, 4, pp. 217–31.

Psacharopoulos, G (ed.) (1987) *Economics of Education: research and studies.* Oxford, Pergamon.

Putnam, R (1993) *Making Democracy Work: civic traditions in modern Italy.* Princeton, NJ, Princeton University Press.

Quintas, P (2002) 'Managing knowledge in a new century', pp. 1–14 in S Little, P Quintas and T Ray (eds) *Managing Knowledge: an essential reader.* London, Sage.

Raggatt, P (1993) 'Post-Fordism and distance education: a flexible strategy for change'. *Open Learning*, 8, 1, pp. 21–31.

Ram, G (1989) *Going Modular.* London, Council for National Academic Awards.

Ranson, S (1998) 'Lineages of the learning society', pp. 1–24 in S Ranson (ed), *Inside the Learning Society*, London, Cassell.

Rees, T (1992) *Women and the Labour Market*. London, Routledge.

Revans, R (1982) *The Origins and Growth of Action Learning*. Lund, Studentlitteratur.

Roberts, D, Higgins, T and Lloyd, R (1992) *Higher Education: the student experience*. Leeds, HEIST.

Rogers, A (1996) *Teaching Adults*. Buckingham, Open University Press, second edition.

Rogers, C et al. (1983) *Freedom to Learn for the 80s*. Columbus, OH, Charles Merrill.

Rogers, J (2001) *Adults Learning*. Buckingham, Open University Press, fourth edition.

Romiszowski, A (1990) 'Trends in corporate training and development', pp. 17–48 in M Mulder, A Romiszowski and P van der Sijde (eds) *Strategic Human Resource Development*. Amsterdam, Swets and Zeitlinger.

Rumble, G (1989) ' "Open learning", "distance learning", and the misuse of language'. *Open Learning*, 4, 2, pp. 28–36.

Rumble, G (1995) 'Labour market theories and distance education 1: industrialisation and distance education'. *Open Learning*, 10, 1, pp. 10–20.

Rumble, G (2001) 'Re-inventing distance education, 1971–2001'. *International Journal of Lifelong Education*, 20, 1/1, pp. 31–43.

Sargant, N, Field, J, Francis, H, Schuller, T and Tuckett, A (1997) *The Learning Divide*. Leicester, National Institute of Adult Continuing Education.

Schied, F, Howell, S, Carter, V and Preston, J (1998) 'Creating contingency workers: a critical study of the learning organisation', pp. 280–90 in J Holford, P Jarvis and C Griffin (eds) *International Perspectives on Lifelong Learning*. London, Kogan Page.

Schön, D (1988) *Educating the Reflective Practitioner*. San Francisco, CA, Jossey-Bass.

Schuller, T (2001) 'The complementary roles of human and social capital'. *Isuma*, 2, 1, pp. 18–24.

Schultz, T (1961) 'Investment in human capital'. *American Economic Review*, 51, 1, pp. 1–17.

Schultz, T (1971) *Investment in Human Capital: the role of education and of research*. New York, Free Press.

Scottish Education Department (1983) *Education in the Community*. Edinburgh, HMSO.

Selwyn, N, Gorard, S, and Williams, S (2001) 'The role of the "technical fix" in UK lifelong education policy'. *International Journal of Lifelong Education*, 20, 4, pp. 255–71.

Senge, P (1990) *The Fifth Discipline: the art and practice of the learning organisation*. New York, Doubleday.

Shale, D (1990) 'Toward a reconceptualisation of distance education', pp. 331–43 in M Moore, P Cookson, J Donaldson and B Quigley (eds) *Contemporary Issues in American Distance Education*. Oxford, Pergamon.

Shale, D and Garrison, D (1990) 'Education and communication', pp. 23–39 in D Garrison and D Shale (eds) *Education at a Distance: from issues to practice*. Malabar, FL, Robert Krieger.

Shuttleworth, D (1993) *Enterprise Learning in Action: education and economic renewal for the twenty-first century*. London, Routledge.

Simosko, S (1991) *Accreditation of Prior Learning: a practical guide for professionals*. London, Kogan Page.

Sinclair, M (1991) 'Women, work and skill: economic theories and feminist perspectives', pp. 1–24 in M Redclift and M Sinclair (eds), *Working Women: international perspectives on labour and gender ideology*. London, Routledge.

Sloboda, J (1986) 'What is skill?' pp. 16–25 in A Gellatly (ed.) *The Skilful Mind: an introduction to cognitive psychology*. Milton Keynes, Open University Press.

Smith, P and Kelly, M (eds) (1987) *Distance Education and the Mainstream: convergence in education*. London, Croom Helm.

Smithers, A and Griffin, A (1986) *The Progress of Mature Students*. Manchester, Joint Matriculation Board.

Smithers, A and Robinson, P (1989) *Increasing Participation in Higher Education*. London, BP Educational Services.

Smithers, A and Robinson, P (2000) 'Colleges in the new millennium', pp. 191–208 in A Smithers and P Robinson (eds) *Further Education Re-formed*. London, Falmer.

Spencer, L and Taylor, S (1994) *Participation and Progress in the Labour Market: key issues for women*. Sheffield, Employment Department.

Squires, G (1986) *Modularisation*. Manchester, CONTACT.

Squires, G (1987) *The Curriculum Beyond School*. London, Hodder and Stoughton.

Squires, G (1990) *First Degree: the Undergraduate Curriculum*. Milton Keynes, Open University Press.

Stephenson, J (1992) 'Capability and quality in higher education', pp. 1–9 in J Stephenson and S Weil (eds) *Quality in Learning: a capability approach in higher education*. London, Kogan Page.

Stephenson, J and Weil, S (1992) 'Four themes in educating for capability', pp. 10–18 in J Stephenson and S Weil (eds) *Quality in Learning: a capability approach in higher education*. London, Kogan Page.

Stewart, J and McGoldrick, J (eds) (1996) *Human Resource Development: perspectives, strategies and practice*. London, Pitman.

Straker, G (ed.) (2000) *Conceptions of Self-directed Learning: theoretical and conceptual considerations*. Munster, Waxman.

Stuart, M (2000) 'Beyond rhetoric: reclaiming a radical agenda for active participation in higher education', pp. 23–35 in J Thompson (ed) *Stretching the Academy: the politics and practice of widening participation in higher education*. Leicester, National Institute of Adult Continuing Education.

Szreter, S (2000) 'Social capital, the economy, and education in historical perspective', pp. 56–77 in S Baron, J Field, and T Schuller (eds) *Social Capital: critical perspectives*. Oxford, Oxford University Press.

Tait, A (ed.) (1993) *Key Issues in Open Learning: a reader. An anthology from the journal Open Learning, 1986–1992*. Harlow, Longman.

Tait, J, and Knight, P (eds) (1996) *The Management of Independent Learning*. London, Kogan Page.

Tasker, M and Packham, D (1994) 'Changing cultures? Government intervention in higher education 1987–93'. *British Journal of Educational Studies*, 42, 2, pp. 150–62.

Taylor, P (1993) *The Texts of Paulo Freire*. Buckingham, Open University Press.

Taylor, R (2000) 'Concepts of self-directed learning in higher education: re-establishing the democratic tradition', pp. 68–79 in J Thompson (ed.) *Stretching the Academy: the politics and practice of widening participation in higher education*. Leicester, National Institute of Adult Continuing Education.

Tennant, M (1988) *Psychology and Adult Learning*. London, Routledge, second edition.

Thirlwall, A (1994) *Growth and Development: with special reference to developing economies*. London, Macmillan, fifth edition.

Thomas, A (1991) *Beyond Education: a new perspective on society's management of learning*. San Francisco, CA, Jossey-Bass.

Thomas, D (ed.) (1995) *Flexible Learning Strategies in Higher and Further Education*. London, Cassell.

Thomas, J (1982) *Radical Adult Education: theory and practice*. Nottingham, University of Nottingham, Department of Adult Education.

Thomas, L (2001) *Widening Participation in Post-compulsory Education*. London, Continuum.

Thompson, J (ed.) (2000) *Stretching the Academy: the politics and practice of widening participation in higher education*. Leicester, National Institute of Adult Continuing Education.

Thomson, R and Mabey, C (1994) *Developing Human Resources*. Oxford, Butterworth-Heinemann.

Thorpe, M and Grugeon, D (eds) (1987) *Open Learning for Adults*. Harlow, Longman.

Tight, M (ed.) (1983) *Adult Learning and Education*. London, Croom Helm.

Tight, M (1993) 'Access, not access courses: maintaining a broad vision', pp. 62–74 in R Edwards, S Sieminski and D Zeldin (eds) *Adult Learners, Education and Training*. London, Routledge.

Tight, M (1994) 'Utopia and the education of adults'. *International Journal of University Adult Education*, 33, 2, pp. 29–44.

Tight, M (1995) 'Education, work and adult life: a literature review'. *Research Papers in Education*, 10, 3, pp. 381–98.

Tight, M (1996) *Key Concepts in Adult Education and Training*. London, Routledge.

Tight, M (1998a) 'Lifelong learning: opportunity or compulsion?' *British Journal of Educational Studies*, 46, 3, pp. 251–63.

Tight, M (1998b) 'Education, education, education! The vision of lifelong learning in the Kennedy, Dearing and Fryer reports'. *Oxford Review of Education*, 24, 4, pp. 473–85.

Tight, M (1998c) 'Bridging the "learning divide": the nature and politics of participation'. *Studies in the Education of Adults*, 30, 2, pp. 110–19.

Tinto, V (1987) *Leaving College: rethinking the causes and cures of student attrition*. Chicago, IL, University of Chicago Press.

Titmus, C (1999) 'Concepts and practices of education and adult education: obstacles to lifelong education and lifelong learning?' *International Journal of Lifelong Education*, 18, 5, pp. 343–54.

Toffler, A (1970) *Future Shock*. London, Bodley Head.

Tough, A (1971) *The Adult's Learning Projects: a fresh approach to theory and practice in adult learning*. Toronto, Ontario Institute for Studies in Education.

Tough, A (1989) 'Self-directed learning: concepts and practice', pp. 256–60 in C Titmus (ed.) *Lifelong Education for Adults: an international handbook*. Oxford, Pergamon.

Tovey, P (1994) *Quality Assurance in Continuing Professional Education: an analysis*. London, Routledge.

Training Agency (1989) *Enterprise in Higher Education: key features of the proposals 1988–89*. Sheffield, Training Agency.

Training Agency (1990) *Enterprise in Higher Education: key features of the proposals 1989–90*. Sheffield, Training Agency.

Tucker, V (1999) 'The myth of development: a critique of a Eurocentric discourse', pp. 1–26 in R Munck and D O'Hearn (eds) *Critical Development Theory: contributions to a new paradigm*. London, Zed Books.

Tuijnman, A (1989) *Recurrent Education, Earnings and Well-being: a fifty year longitudinal study of a cohort of Swedish men*. Stockholm, Almqvist & Wiksell.

Tuijnman, A (ed.) (1996) *International Encyclopedia of Adult Education and Training*. Oxford, Pergamon, second edition.

Tynjala, P (1997) 'Developing education students' conceptions of the learning process in different learning environments'. *Learning and Instruction*, 7, 3, pp. 277–92.

Unit for the Development of Adult Continuing Education (1989) *Understanding Competence: a development paper*. Leicester, UDACE.

Usher, R, Bryant, I and Johnston, R (1997) *Adult Education and the Postmodern Challenge: learning beyond the limits*. London, Routledge.

Usher, R and Edwards, R (1994) *Postmodernism and Education*. London, Routledge.

Verduin, J and Clark, T (1991) *Distance Education: the foundations of effective practice*. San Francisco, CA, Jossey-Bass.

Vroeijenstijn, A (1995) *Improvement and Accountability: navigating between Scylla and Charybdis. Guide for external quality assessment in higher education*. London, Jessica Kingsley.

Wade, W, Hodgkinson, K, Smith, A and Arfield, J (eds) (1994) *Flexible Learning in Higher Education*. London, Kogan Page.

Wain, K (1993) 'Lifelong education and adult education: the state of the theory'. *International Journal of Lifelong Education*, 12, 2, pp. 86–99.

Walker, L (1994) 'The new higher education systems, modularity and student capability', pp. 24–42 in A Jenkins and L Walker (eds) *Developing Student Capability Through Modular Courses*. London, Kogan Page.

Ward, K and Taylor, R (eds) (1986) *Adult Education and the Working Class: education for the missing millions*. London, Croom Helm.

Watkins, K (1991) 'Many voices: defining human resource development from different disciplines'. *Adult Education Quarterly*, 41, 4, pp. 241–55.

Watkins, K and Marsick, V (1992) 'Building the learning organisation: a new role for human resource developers'. *Studies in Continuing Education*, 14, 2, pp. 115–29.

Watson, D, Brooks, J, Coghill, C, Lindsay, R and Scurry, D (1989) *Managing the Modular Course: perspectives from Oxford Polytechnic*. Milton Keynes, Open University Press.

Weil, S (1986) 'Non-traditional learners within traditional higher education institutions: discovery and disappointment'. *Studies in Higher Education*, 11, 3, pp. 219–35.

Weil, S and McGill, I (eds) (1989) *Making Sense of Experiential Learning: diversity in theory and practice*. Milton Keynes, Open University Press.

Wenger, E (2000) 'Communities of practice and social learning systems'. *Organization*, 7, 2, pp. 225–46.

Williams, K (1994) 'Vocationalism and liberal education: exploring the tensions'. *Journal of the Philosophy of Education*, 28, 1, pp. 89–100.

Williams, R (1988) *Keywords: a vocabulary of culture and society*. London, Fontana (first edition 1976).

Wilson, J (ed.) (1999) *Human Resource Development: learning and training for individuals and organizations*. London, Kogan Page.

Wiltshire, H (1956) 'The great tradition in university adult education'. *Adult Education*, 29, 2, pp. 88–97.

Winch, C and Gingell, J (1999) *Key Concepts in the Philosophy of Education*. London, Routledge.

Wolf, A (1995) *Competence-based Assessment*. Buckingham, Open University Press.

Woodhall, M (1987) 'Human capital concepts', pp. 21–4 in G Psacharopoulos (ed.) *Economics of Education: research and studies*. Oxford, Pergamon.

Woodley, A and Parlett, M (1983) 'Student drop-out'. *Teaching at a Distance*, 24, pp. 2–23.

Working Group on Vocational Qualifications (1986) *Review of Vocational Qualifications in England and Wales*. London, HMSO.

Wright, P (1991) 'Access or accessibility'. *Journal of Access Studies*, 6, 1, pp. 6–15.

Yorke, M (1999) *Leaving Early: undergraduate non-completion in higher education*. London, Falmer.

Young, M (1998) *The Curriculum of the Future: from the 'new sociology of education' to a critical theory of learning*. London, Falmer.

Zuber-Skerritt, O and Ryan, Y (eds) (1994) *Quality in Postgraduate Education*. London, Kogan Page.

Index

Printed in the United Kingdom
by Lightning Source UK Ltd.
106742UKS00001B/44